"*Being Claimed by the Eucharist* \. for priests and deacons but is also applicable to all people of faith. It describes theology from above as an approach that encourages the faithful to ongoing conversion and ongoing formation, while theology from below engages reality as experienced in actual ministry with its emotional, psychological, and spiritual dimensions. The concept of 'being given for others' connects the roles of the ordained to the people of God by linking the Eucharist and discipleship. An emphasis on brokenness stresses the need for the redemptive power of the cross through which God's love becomes transformative grace. The author's goal, which is to convey and illuminate the importance of the role of ministry in the life of the church, is admirably achieved."

—Katarina Schuth, OSF, Professor Emerita, St. Paul Seminary at the University of St. Thomas

"The Second Vatican Council reminded us clearly that the celebration of the Eucharist is the 'source and summit' of our lives of faith. In this wonderfully engaging book, Scott Detisch invites us to relearn and live the story of this central celebration of the mystery of divine love, which calls us together to receive and be the Body of Christ in our world. This is a must-read meditation for ordained ministers of the Eucharist, especially for those who preside at the Eucharist, but there is indeed something in this book for all the baptized. Readers are sure to be renewed in their eucharistic spirituality!"

—Daniel P. Horan, OFM, Director of the Center for Spirituality, Saint Mary's College, Notre Dame, Indiana

Being Claimed by
the Eucharist We Celebrate

*A Spiritual Narrative for
Priests and Deacons*

Scott P. Detisch

LITURGICAL PRESS
Collegeville, Minnesota

www.litpress.org

Scripture texts in this work are taken from the *New American Bible, revised edition* © 2010, 1991, 1986, 1970 Confraternity of Christian Doctrine, Washington, DC and are used by permission of the copyright owner. All Rights Reserved. No part of the New American Bible may be reproduced in any form without permission in writing from the copyright owner.

Excerpts from the English translation of General Instruction, Non-Biblical Readings from *The Liturgy of the Hours* © 1973, 1974, 1975, International Commission on English in the Liturgy Corporation (ICEL); excerpts from the English translation of *Rites of Ordination of a Bishop, of Priests, and of Deacons* © 2000, 2002, ICEL; excerpts from the English translation of *The Roman Missal* © 2010, ICEL. All rights reserved.

1	2	3	4	5	6	7	8	9

Library of Congress Cataloging-in-Publication Data

Names: Detisch, Scott P., author.
Title: Being claimed by the Eucharist we celebrate : a spiritual narrative for priests and deacons / Scott P. Detisch.
Description: Collegeville, Minnesota : Liturgical Press, [2022] | Summary: "Fr. Detisch explores a spirituality of holy orders through the eucharistic actions of Christ: take, bless, break, and give"— Provided by publisher.
Identifiers: LCCN 2021038891 (print) | LCCN 2021038892 (ebook) | ISBN 9780814666975 (paperback) | ISBN 9780814666982 (epub) | ISBN 9780814666982 (pdf)
Subjects: LCSH: Spiritual life—Catholic Church. | Lord's Supper—Catholic Church. | Priests—Religious life. | Deacons—Religious life.
Classification: LCC BX2350.3 .D48 2022 (print) | LCC BX2350.3 (ebook) | DDC 248.8/94—dc23
LC record available at https://lccn.loc.gov/2021038891
LC ebook record available at https://lccn.loc.gov/2021038892

This book is dedicated to
the wonderful parishioners of
St. John the Evangelist Church
in Girard, PA
with whom I have the privilege
of celebrating the Eucharist as their pastor.

This book is written in appreciation and gratitude to
the seminarians, lay and religious students,
faculty, administration, and staff at
St. Mary Seminary and Graduate School of Theology
in Wickliffe, OH
where I have the honor of teaching theology,
but even more,
where I am constantly inspired to keep growing
in my own personal narrative of faith.

Contents

Acknowledgments

I am so indebted to the eucharistic communities in which I have served throughout my years as a priest, but in a special way to my home parish of Our Lady of Peace in Erie, Pennsylvania, where I experienced very early on in my developmental years how the Eucharist was central to the life of any parish. Every parish I have been connected to has had its own unique character and particular ways of celebrating the Eucharist. Yet all of them were communities that were gathered by the Eucharist and sent forth striving and struggling to live the Eucharist in their lives and in their common mission as disciples of Christ. Celebrating the Eucharist with all of these communities has shown me that this central sacrament of our Catholic faith does indeed have the power to claim people's lives, sometimes with great eagerness and enthusiasm, other times with quiet devotion and humble service. These communities have also taught me the importance of celebrating the Eucharist as a priest for them with authenticity, preparedness, energy, and conviction. In essence, they have drawn out from me what I have been called to be for them, reminding me of the implications of what it means to be a priest and an ordinary minister of the Eucharist on their behalf and in their midst. To each of these communities, no matter how briefly or how long I was with them, I am very grateful.

I am also very grateful to the teachers I have had in my life who opened up for me the theological and spiritual depths of the Eucharist. First among them was my sacramental theology professor in seminary, Fr. Xavier Seubert, OFM. His unique style of teaching theology, coupled with his engaging manner of presiding and preaching at the Eucharist, really excited me in a way that made the Eucharist so central to my understanding of church, discipleship, holy orders, and pastoral ministry. In addition, my mentor during my doctoral work, Dr. George S. Worgul Jr. helped me to study with more rigor the theological richness of the Catholic Church's teachings on the Eucharist. Furthermore, George expanded my appreciation of the connections among the Eucharist, our faith in Christ, and the day-to-day dynamics of human living.

While teachers in my life have always inspired me, so too have students I have taught. In recent years, I have been deeply touched by a whole array of students, in particular: seminarians whose intelligent grasp of theology and whose pastoral hearts have now made them effective and energetic priests; laywomen and men whose capacity to connect theology with the day-to-day struggles of discipleship have led them to become well-educated co-workers in the vineyard of the Lord; deacon candidates and their wives in deacon formation programs who sacrificed a lot of personal time so that they could effectively help lead others in the mission of the church; and parishioners who came to adult faith formation sessions I have offered and brought with them a deep desire to grow in their faith and, at the same time, revealed a wealth of insight into the life of faith that they did not always realize they already had. I truly love being a co-learner and co-disciple with and among all these different groups within the church. If I began to list them by name, these acknowledgements would be longer than any chapter in this book. In the same vein I am very grateful to the priests and deacons who have attended seminars and days of recollection in which I have tested out some of the theses I put forth in this book. The insights they offered as well as the questions they asked gave me much more clarity about the direction this book needed to take.

Finally, I am always deeply indebted to the staff at Liturgical Press who have assisted me in my writing in countless ways. The encouragement they have offered me when I have proposed my writing projects has been invaluable. In particular, Peter Dwyer has been enormously helpful in the guidance and feedback he has offered with this book. Working with Peter and with the folks at Liturgical Press has made me a better writer and a clearer thinker.

Prologue

For over a hundred years now, biblical scholars are prone to remark that "a text without context is a pretext." Such a phrase has become an idiomatic warning that it would be so easy to misconstrue the true meaning of a biblical text without knowing the real intent of the author(s) of that text, the operative theology of the author(s), and the denotation of terms and connotation of phrases and images that are found within the text. In short, all that constitutes the context allows us to read rightly and understand properly the text itself. With that in mind, I think it is important to provide some context for the text that follows. I do so by offering some of the operative principles underlying my purpose for writing this book, the theological perspectives that dominate it, the style and focus that permeate the pages you are about to read. There are mainly three guiding principles that would help you grasp the context surrounding the text you are about to read.

1. A Theology from Below

In any theological endeavor there are mainly two different approaches: a theology from above and a theology from below. A theology from above presents an a priori ideal of the subject at hand and is often encapsulated by doctrines that the church formulates. In the case of the sacraments, a theology from above is best found within the very rites of the sacraments themselves informed by church's doctrines. Those rites provide an icon of the sacramentalized identity and way of life for the recipients of the sacrament that is being celebrated. This is no less true of the rituals and theology of holy orders, which figure prominently in this book. The different rites of ordination offer the a priori icon to which every deacon and priest pledges himself to become and the ideal he commits himself to live. One of the important values of a theology-from-above approach is that it constantly beckons us to continue in our journey of ongoing conversion and ongoing formation, because we are never at a point in which we have reached the ideal; yet the Holy Spirit keeps nudging us along.

A theology from below, on the other hand, presents the subject at hand by forthrightly engaging the reality of human existence as it is truly experienced. It is an a posteriori approach that illuminates how the divine meets the existential reality of humanness, thereby revealing how God is with us in what *is* and not merely how God calls us to what *could be* or *should be.* Rather than offering an icon of the ideal, a theology from below offers a portrait of the real, but a very graced portrait at that. Thus, for example, a theology of holy orders from below engages the reality of what ordained deacons and priests actually experience in their exercise of the ministry to which God has called them. Such a theological approach does not ignore but makes central to its project the concrete particularities of a deacon's or priest's lived experience, including its emotional, psychological, and spiritual dimensions. Furthermore, this approach contributes to a fruitful meeting between doctrinal teaching and pastoral ministry. It provides a place for a deacon or priest to process his own inevitable struggles that necessarily happen when the ideal meets the real, when noble aspirations are challenged by human limitations.

In any sound theological presentation, both approaches ought to be used together, though in admittedly different proportions. Some theological presentations will be much more dominantly an approach from above; in others, a theology from below will be more pervasive. In the text that follows, I will make repeated use of a theology-from-above approach as I quote both scriptural and ritual texts and explicate from them what are the noble ideals that beckon us in both the sacraments of the Eucharist and holy orders. However, what is more predominant in this book is a theology from below that seeks to delve into how our real lives and our actual experiences are the best places for us to ponder the meaning of the Eucharist and holy orders. This approach strives to unite the truth about ourselves, our church, and our places of ministry with an understanding of how all of this is all drawn into what we celebrate in the Eucharist and what is claimed by our ordination. It is a portrait of a God-saturated reality and not an emphasis on a God-given ideal.

2. A Focus on the Ordained but not an Exclusion of All the Baptized

No theology of ordination (and certainly no presentation on the Eucharist) can ever be only about the clergy. The very nature of ordination is the self-offering of a man's life vis-à-vis Jesus Christ in service *to all the baptized members of the church* as one who leads them in living out their own baptismal priesthood and service to others. Therefore, although this book is intended for the theological and spiritual edification of deacons and priests, what is stipulated about the ordained in the pages that follow cannot be regarded as exclusive to them. As will be made clearer in chapter 6, what is expected of the ordained amongst the people of God is that they live in such a vivid way what is expected of all the people of God. The ordained ritualize within the Liturgy of the Eucharist what is to animate all the baptized in living as missionary disciples of Jesus.[1] This book hopes to heighten an awareness within clergy of what they need in order to help the people they lead and serve

---

1. Pope Francis states: "Every Christian is a missionary to the extent that he or she has encountered the love of God in Jesus Christ: we no longer say that we are 'disciples' and 'missionaries,' but rather that we are always 'missionary disciples.'" Pope Francis, *The Joy of the Gospel* (*Evangelii Gaudium*) (Vatican City: Libreria Editrice Vaticana, 2013), 120.

become aware of the following: all the baptized are to be engaged in the mission of the church; all the members of the church are called to live as eucharistic disciples of Jesus in their day-to-day lives.

As will be made clear, those ordained to the ministerial priesthood have a particular role to play in evoking what is to be evident in the priesthood of all baptized believers. Ordained priests have a specific responsibility and vocation of pastoral, evangelical, and sacramental leadership that draws out the priesthood of Jesus Christ in all members of the church. Likewise, those ordained to the diaconate have a specific role to play within the church to evoke *diakonia* (i.e., service to the needs of others) from all the people of God. Ordained deacons have a particular vocation to make evident the humble servanthood of Jesus that all the baptized are called to live.

While ordained deacons and priests have prominent and defined roles within the celebration of the Eucharist, what they do liturgically is a mimesis of the roles summoned forth from all the people of God by the Eucharist. Like the mimesis of the prophets in the Old Testament, the gestures, actions, and words of deacons and priests within the Liturgy of the Eucharist demonstrate what all the baptized are to live themselves as people nourished and missioned by the Eucharist. Likewise, since the very essence of the Eucharist is Christ's body and blood being given *for the many,* or *for you,* or *for all* (depending on which scriptural version of the institution narrative one is using), then the links between the Eucharist and holy orders must necessarily involve how deacons and priests give themselves for the people with whom they celebrate the Eucharist and how deacons and priests help to animate in their people their own eucharistic self-giving to others and to the world in which they live. What this means is that any theological and spiritual writing about Eucharist and holy orders can never be some exposition that contributes to clerical identity in and of itself. A text that connects explicitly holy orders to Eucharist connects the diaconate and priesthood explicitly to the dynamic of *being given for* others. Knowing this context is crucial for you as the reader not to see in this book some pretext for clerical Gnosticism in which the ordained alone have access to the ingredients for a higher spiritual life than others. Hence this book that I offer is meant to help priests and deacons recognize the connections between their roles within the Eucharist and their lives *within* and *for* the people of God. This text is intended to deepen the spiritual and theological grasp of the links between the Eucharist and holy orders so that deacons and priests can assist their people in making spiritual and theological links between the Eucharist and their own baptized and confirmed discipleship.

3. An Emphasis on Brokenness

In part 2 of this book, the eucharistic verbs "take," "bless," "break," and "give" are explored; however, it will be evident from the outset that the verb "break" becomes pivotal to the whole exposition of Eucharist and holy orders that is offered. While there is a decided emphasis on the concepts of "breaking" and "brokenness," this is not a fatalistic text that is obsessed with all that is wrong with the world, with the church, with clergy, or with human life in general. It is also not a *via negativa* approach to understanding the Eucharist or holy orders: that is, it does not offer a theology from the viewpoints of everything that these sacraments are not achieving in the church right now or everything that they are not meant to be. While this book will be forthright in naming the brokenness of the church, the world, the lives of our people, and the lives of deacons and priests, it is not a dark and dour text about ordained ministry, the state of our liturgical celebrations, nor the reality of our church and parishes.

Instead, consistent with a theology-from-below approach, the emphasis in this treatise on breaking and brokenness takes seriously the redemptive power of the cross of Christ. The passion and death of the Incarnate Son of God is the point of divinity's full communion with every dimension of humanity's brokenness. It is the place where God's complete self-emptying in love becomes transformative grace being poured into each and every wound of our human condition. Such an approach necessarily needs to name forthrightly the wounds of our church that have been ignored for too long and cannot be excluded any longer from any theological and spiritual presentation of the sacraments that are at her very core. A focus on the breaking that occurs within the Eucharist must take seriously the brokenness in our parishes, places of ministry, and the lives of the people whom deacons and priests serve. Finally, seeing the verb "break" as central to what both the Eucharist and holy orders mean cannot help but to see one's personal brokenness and the brokenness in one's ministerial life as a potent place of intimacy with Christ—a place of meeting that cannot and ought not to be circumvented or dismissed in one's desire to live authentically as a deacon or priest.

It is my hope that what I offer in this book will contribute to a renewed appreciation of the defining role that the Eucharist plays within the ministry of priests and deacons because it defines the life of the whole church. Furthermore, I want this text to speak to deacons and priests who are hurting, discouraged, or depleted for any number of reasons: the abuse scandals in the church, the problems in one's place of ministry, the difficulties in one's personal life, the frustrations and failures in one's own ministerial life. By engaging you as a priest or deacon at the level of what you are actually experiencing (and not what you ideally ought to be), I am striving to offer some assistance to your spiritual growth and ministerial renewal in and through the Eucharist. It is my prayer that the pages that follow are worthy of your desire for that growth and renewal.

Part One

"Narrative Grace" within the Sacraments of the Eucharist and Holy Orders

chapter one

The Eucharist as a Narrative

"The significance—and ultimately the quality—of the work we do is determined by our understanding of the story in which we are taking part."

—Wendell Berry[1]

In the 2006 film *Stranger Than Fiction,* the main character, Howard Crick, an IRS auditor leading a rather boring life of routine, begins to hear voices, more specifically, a single voice at different times throughout his day. He realizes that the voice is actually narrating the actions and events currently unfolding in his life. Shortly thereafter Howard watches an award-winning author being interviewed on television and discovers that the voice he has been hearing belongs to that author, Karen Eiffel. After some time of listening to Karen's voice narrating his life, Howard hears her say something that ominously signals his impending death. Frantically Howard tries to find Karen in order to change the plot in the story and spare his life.

While this film certainly falls into the category of "dark comedy," it does cause one to think: Who really is the author of our

---

1. Wendell Berry, "Christianity and the Survival of Creation," *Cross Currents* 43, no. 2 (Summer 1993): 149. This essay later appears in Berry's book *Sex, Economy, Freedom & Community: Eight Essays* (Berkeley, CA: Counterpoint, 1992).

lives? The advertising for this film includes the following tag line: "Everybody knows that your life is a story. But what if a story was your life?"[2] Each of us has a life story made up of many different narrative elements—our place of origin, our family, our circles of friends, the major influences in our lives, those we have loved, the places we have lived and gone to school and worked, our genetic and physiological make-up, our hobbies and interests, our beliefs and convictions; the list could go on and on. Yet underneath all of these details, who or what truly generates how the plot unfolds? Is each of us, with our own free will and power of self-determination, the primary author of our story? Or has Someone Else been "authoring" us all along, drawing all the particulars of our lives into a story that is our true narrative?

Philosophical theologians will rightly point out that the answer to these questions is some combination of the two abovementioned options. But I think we ought not dismiss too quickly how much God lovingly seeks to author our lives by drawing us into a story— a narrative that is, at the same time, already written and seeking to be composed. What do I mean by this? On the one hand, God, as our Creator, sets in motion the story of our lives and allows our free will to play a key role in how that story will unfold, how it will be written. On the other hand, God, as our Savior, is the Word, and as that Word is the narrative of God's love that has already been written and that strives to claim and shape the very plotline and destiny of our own personal story. These may seem like musings that are "stranger than fiction," but the point is for us to recognize that, when we are born and baptized, we are not blank pages on which we can sketch any possible plotline that we want for our lives. We are born and baptized into the grace of the Holy Spirit, who draws us into the sacred story of Jesus Christ. We will explore how that story of Jesus is essentially a eucharistic

---

2. *Stranger Than Fiction*, directed by Marc Forster (Los Angeles: Columbia Pictures, 2006), https://www.imdb.com/title/tt0420223.

story, which seeks to claim every aspect of our personal story as men of faith and as ordained deacons and priests.

While God might be the main author of our personal narrative, we play an important role as co-authors. Therefore, it is incumbent on us to recognize that there are many different components within the story of our lives—some competing with each other for greater attention. As co-authors with God, we need to allow ourselves to be shaped by the aspects of our story that we value the most. These include the many characters, settings, plot twists, conflicts, and resolutions that have shaped our lives. However, the most deeply operative narrative of our lives cannot merely arise unreflectively out of all of these narrative elements. In short, the story of our lives cannot merely happen to us, as it does for the unreflective person; it must be chosen; it must be lived. As men of Christian faith, we need to allow the story of Jesus Christ to become the most operative and compelling story within our own story.

As men of the church, when we were ordained deacons and priests, we came forward with a narrative of personal faith arising from our particular background in which we experienced a specific religious vocation. We were most likely captivated by the story lines of deacons and priests we admired. Years beforehand, we were sacramentally initiated into the narrative of the Catholic Church that drew us into an inspiring tale of over two thousand years of Christian discipleship and conviction. But, to use the words of Wendell Berry, "the significance—and ultimately the quality—of the work we do"[3] as deacons and priests needs to be shaped very specifically by the eucharistic narrative of Jesus Christ. As deacons and priests, the Eucharist is at the center of our work (our ministry). Not only do we celebrate the Eucharist often, but so much of our identities and lives as men sacramentally configured to Christ the Deacon and Christ the Priest are eucharistic in nature. The same is true of the life and identity of Jesus Christ.

---

3. Berry, "Christianity and the Survival of Creation," 149.

He did not merely institute the Eucharist at a certain point in his public ministry; his very incarnation is eucharistic. This is an important principle underlying the following pages. Therefore, just as the narrative of Jesus is eucharistic, so also the narrative of every deacon and priest ought to be eucharistic.

In explaining the significance of the eucharistic prayer, the *General Instruction of the Roman Missal* (*GIRM*) labels as one of the prayer's chief elements the "Institution narrative and Consecration."[4] In explaining this crucial element of the liturgy, noted sacramental theologian Fr. Paul Turner writes: "In the heart of the Eucharistic Prayer, the priest tells the story of the Last Supper."[5] Our tradition has handed on to us a paradigmatic narrative of what Jesus said, did, and offered at a final meal shared with his disciples on the day before he died. But the story of the Last Supper, coming near the end of Jesus' life, reveals the underlying narrative that has been told by the entire life of the Incarnate Son of God. What follows in this book is premised on how the key eucharistic actions of Jesus within the institution narrative—*take, bless, break, give*—define the whole story line of the Word-made-flesh: he *takes* on human flesh and all that humanness entails; he *blesses* God the Father and the people of God with what he lives; in his complete self-giving Jesus is *broken* by his embrace of the brokenness of the sinful human condition and by the cruel suffering and death inflicted on him; then he *gives* everything about himself for the salvation of the world—his body and blood, his humanity and divinity, his living and dying, his Sacred Heart and his Holy Spirit. Therefore, the entirety of Jesus' life is the narrative that institutes the Eucharist. This is why the assertion can be made that the meal with his disciples at the *end* of Jesus' life actually reveals the meaning and mission of his *entire* life. Likewise, this meal reveals the meaning and mission of the life of every disciple

---

4. *General Instruction of the Roman Missal* (2007), 79d.

5. Paul Turner, *Let Us Pray: A Guide to the Rubrics of Sunday Mass; Updated to Conform with the Revised English Translation of The Roman Missal* (Collegeville, MN: Liturgical Press, 2012), no. 565, p. 115.

who is fed by the Eucharist. In receiving Christ in the Eucharist, all disciples receive the eucharistic narrative of the entire life of Jesus Christ, a narrative with a mission.[6]

As with any narrative, there is a plot that unfolds in a definitive sequence of events; it has a certain chronology. The plot of the Eucharist is defined by the series of key words within the institution narrative—*take, bless, break, give*. As a sacred narrative infused with the power of grace, the sequence of these plot elements not only defines the identity and mission of Jesus, it also draws into the narrative all those who celebrate the Eucharist. This is the power of "narrative grace" within the Eucharist.[7] With that in mind, we can recognize that Jesus offers *to us* the grace-infused eucharistic narrative so that the Eucharist can then reveal *in us* the ever-present story of Jesus and bring forth the true story of our own lives.

There is no more crucial prayer than the Eucharist; it is the place of greatest intimacy with Christ and, therefore, the true defining element of our spiritual lives. Moreover, since as priests and deacons we celebrate the Eucharist quite often (daily for most priests), it is not only a vital experience of prayer and an oft repeated ritual in our lives; it is to be the rich source of God's power and grace that lays hold of us (including our deepest selves) and writes the story line of our lives. This narrative grace works slowly throughout the unfolding of the plot points within our story. The Eucharist is meant to transform us bit by bit over time, shaping everything we

---

6. As mentioned in the prologue, the eucharistic narrative claims all the baptized followers of Christ, not just the ordained. However, this text will explore mostly the claims that the Eucharist makes on the lives of deacons and priests as ordinary ministers of the Eucharist. I hope that any reader who is not a deacon or priest might see in this book the parallel claims that the Eucharist makes on her or his own life as a committed disciple of Jesus.

7. I use this term in order to capture more effectively the theological assertion that the story of Jesus, as well as his Last Supper, are not mere tales that we read, listen to, or ritualize and imitate. Filled with the power of God's grace, the story of Jesus unites those who read it, listen to it, and ritualize it to the person of Jesus and to the story line that has defined his public life and ministry, including his death and resurrection.

do and everything we offer in our ministry as well as how we do it and how we offer it. In short, the Eucharist, so filled with narrative grace, claims everything about us because it is to be the defining story of our lives. This book will examine the narrative grace that operates within the sequential story line that the Eucharist writes within our lives as it intersects with the narrative of holy orders. In the pages that follow we will examine how the Eucharist defines what it means for us as ordained deacons and priests to *take, bless, break,* and *give,* not merely as ritual gestures, but as the unfolding plot within the narrative of our lives and ministries. Each of us knows that our life as an ordained man has been a story; yet all along there has been a eucharistic story that has been our life. To paraphrase Wendell Berry, "the significance—and ultimately the quality"—of the ministry we do as deacons and priests is determined by our understanding of this story in which we are taking part. Let us now turn to the narrative elements of that story.

Eucharistic Spirituality in a Time of Brokenness

> *And it happened that, while [Jesus] was with them at table, he took bread, said the blessing, broke it, and gave it to them. With that their eyes were opened and they recognized him, but he vanished from their sight. Then they said to each other, "Were not our hearts burning [within us] while he spoke to us on the way and opened the scriptures to us?" So they set out at once and returned to Jerusalem where they found gathered together the eleven and those with them who were saying, "The Lord has truly been raised and has appeared to Simon!" Then the two recounted what had taken place on the way and how he was made known to them in the breaking of the bread.*
>
> —Luke 24:30-35[8]

---

8. All Scripture quotes are taken from the *New American Bible Revised Edition* unless otherwise noted, since this is the translation that deacons and priests use most often in their liturgical roles.

The Eucharist within the New Testament was often identified as "the breaking of the bread."[9] In the Last Supper accounts from Paul and the Synoptic writers, it is *broken* bread that Jesus refers to as "my body."[10] Therefore, it should not be a surprise to us that any attempt to articulate the spirituality of the Eucharist needs to arise out of the experience of brokenness. Brokenness is a key narrative element of the Eucharist. It is important to note, therefore, that the ideas for this book surfaced soon after the painful Pennsylvania grand jury report of sexual abuse within the church, which included a shocking exposé of the perfidious behavior of some clergymen. This report sent many people into a tailspin of confusion and despair, wondering not only how this could happen, but, more painfully, how could such predatory behavior be carried out by men ordained for such sacred duties. This gnawing question became like a taped recording that was set on a continuous loop inside of our heads. Over and over again, we kept asking ourselves, perhaps too afraid or too ashamed to ask it out loud: How could anyone who regularly celebrates revered rituals justify such vile actions? So many notions of holy orders had become shattered; so many people's confidence in the church had been lost; so many believers, already hovering at the edges of commitment, walked away from the Eucharist.

The Emmaus passage quoted above recounts another time of shattered notions and lost confidence in things that once seemed so sure. In Luke's gospel, we find Cleopas and his unnamed companion walking away from Jerusalem toward the village of Emmaus, after the excruciating disappointment they felt when Jesus was crucified. We can hear the anguish in their voices when they admit to their unrecognized Guest that they "had been hoping that [Jesus] would be the one to redeem Israel" (Luke 24:21). Like those devoted followers of Christ, so many of us have been left wandering and wondering if there is any reason to have hope again—hope that the victims of abuse could ever be healed and

9. See Acts 2:42 and 20:7.
10. See 1 Cor 11:24 and Matt 26:26, among others.

that the church itself (including the priesthood) could ever be redeemed from the devastating effects of this recurring scandal. Most assuredly, as with Cleopas and the other disciple, Jesus meets us in our anguish, sadness, and pain; he receives what lies so painfully inside of us; and he draws us closer to himself through the actions of breaking open the Word with us and then taking, blessing, breaking, and giving us the bread of new life. In short, Jesus meets us in the Eucharist and seeks to transform our hearts so that they burn again with joy and hope, conviction and devotion. Our eucharistic encounters with Christ need to bring us back to our own Jerusalem, that is, to our own original place of strong belief and deep awe about who Jesus is and what his real presence in the Eucharist offers. We need to return to the Jerusalem of our original excitement and enthusiasm over the role we priests and deacons have within the ritual celebration of the Eucharist. Not only will this lead us to an eventual renewal of our ministry as ordained servant-leaders within the church, it will also continue the ongoing conversion that needs to happen within each one of us as disciples of Christ and men of the church.

Another defining experience of brokenness underlying the composition of this book is that great progress was made in writing it during the coronavirus pandemic that sequestered all of us for many weeks in our homes, rectories, and places of residence. The mandated "stay at home" restrictions issued by public officials in the first few months of the pandemic brought about a painful lack and limitation of the communal celebration of the Eucharist for a long time. To celebrate the Eucharist physically all alone seemed to strain the very actions and meaning of *taking, blessing, breaking* bread with a gathered community of disciples of Christ and then *giving* them the body and blood of our Lord. So instead, we priests (with a deacon by our side, in many cases) faithfully celebrated the Eucharist privately, *taking* into our prayers the many lives lost due to the pandemic, the many homes plunged into grief by the sudden death of loved ones, and the many individuals whose isolation brought them great fear, anxiety, and loneliness. We *blessed* God for the heroic doctors, nurses, health care and hospital workers, first responders, essential employees, and the many others who put their own lives at risk to come to the aid of people in need. We *broke* the bread and *poured* the wine of the body and blood of Christ the true servant and priest who helped us hold within our hearts a world broken by a pandemic, but also a world in which so much compassion was being poured out. Finally, we *gave* ourselves to newly (for many of us) embraced forms of ministry via social media that offered hope and comfort to our isolated people—hope and comfort that came from our own eucharistic intimacy with Christ. Like Cleopas and the unnamed disciple walking the road to Emmaus in confusion and despair, our own private eucharistic encounters with Christ restored our hope and trust in him and energized us, as it energized them, to let others know that Jesus is very much alive and with us. In short, our daily, private Emmaus encounters, in which we could not celebrate the Eucharist *with our people*, allowed our lives and ministry to take on the very contours of the Eucharist *for our people*.

These experiences teach us that it is precisely out of brokenness that the power of the Eucharist can be revealed. One cannot take the verb "break" out of the eucharistic narrative and still call it the Eucharist. In addition, these difficult recent experiences in the church also make evident that the Eucharist, as with any sacrament, can never be reduced only to its ritual celebration. The whole purpose of the ritual is that it claims us in order to transform us and inflame us for our mission, as happened with Cleopas and his unidentified companion. The nature of that "claiming" and eucharistic "missioning" will be explored in this book. In the pages ahead, we will look at the liturgical actions of the Eucharist that are a crucial part of the ministry of deacons and priests. Underlying those liturgical actions has to be what Professor Tom Whelan calls "ritual truth." He writes: " 'Ritual truth' occurs when the surface level of a rite carries participants to its deeper structure."[11] Thus,

---

11. Tom Whelan, "Presiding at Eucharist: The *Ars Celebrandi,*" in *Priesthood Today: Ministry in a Changing Church*, ed. Eamonn Conway (Dublin: Veritas Publications, 2013), 327.

the very eucharistic actions of taking, blessing, breaking, and giving on the surface level of the liturgy need to lay hold of deacons and priests at the core of who they are, and draw them into deeper layers of encounter with Christ, whose whole life and ministry exemplified the meaning of the Eucharist.

The Deeper Meaning of the Eucharist

> *The cup of blessing that we bless, is it not a participation in the blood of Christ?*
> *The bread that we break, is it not a participation in the body of Christ?*
>
> —1 Corinthians 10:16

The danger of celebrating any ritual with regularity, even something as sublimely sacred as the Eucharist, is that it can easily slip from being a ritual to becoming a routine. Even when a liturgical rite is approached with great energy and enthusiasm, one can focus too much on the external details of the celebration and never plumb the depths of meaning underneath the surface. All priests and deacons who celebrate the Liturgy of the Eucharist with great regularity ought to hear well Jesus' dire warning about the Pharisees when, quoting the prophet Isaiah, he says of them: "This people honors me with their lips, but their hearts are far from me." (Matt 15:8). As any student of liturgy learns, sacramental ritual is based upon the ancient principle of *lex orandi, lex credendi,* which asserts that what we do within a ritual demonstrates the underlying beliefs that inform what we do, how we do it, and why we are doing it. What we say with our lips ought to express the faith and conviction in our hearts. Our participation in the Eucharist as deacons and priests needs to claim our sense of being a deacon or priest, indeed our sense of who we are as disciples of Christ.

What does it mean for any Christian to *participate in* the Eucharist or, as St. Paul phrases it to the Corinthians, to participate in the body and blood of Christ? Furthermore, what does it mean for any priest or deacon to *participate in* the wonderful celebration of the Eucharist, day in and day out? It means so much more than only engaging in the words and actions of the ritual of the Eucharist and receiving the body and blood of Christ. The Greek word in this Pauline text is *koinonia,* which best translates as having "deep and abiding communion" with another.

The context of the passage from 1 Corinthians quoted above is important: Paul is scolding some of the Corinthians for their participation in Roman meals in which the food had been sacrificed to at least one of the Roman gods, most likely the emperor. This sacrificial act renders that food a supposed means of access to that idol. Therefore, Paul is warning them that they participate in what they eat; that is, they are assenting to enter into communion with the whole system of meaning and belief surrounding what the food within that pagan meal symbolizes. Such assent violates their religious beliefs.

In the Jewish world of meaning, to eat food is to enter into the covenant with God since all food was considered a gift from God's creation. In the Christian world of meaning, to eat and drink the bread and wine of the Lord's Supper is to enter into the very personhood of Jesus Christ, including all that is contained in his identity, his public ministry, his passion, death, resurrection, and glory that transformed all human life and the entire world.

As our tradition teaches, the Eucharist draws us into deep communion with all that the body and blood of Christ are about, which means all that the real presence of Christ consists of, including the inherently transformative power of Christ's death and resurrection. As ordinary (ordained) ministers of communion, the eucharistic actions of priests and deacons in the liturgy are to claim everything about their identity, everything about their inner lives, everything about their outward ministry to the people of God, and everything about their visible lives and actions as men of God. Simply put: *the Eucharist is constantly to transform priests and deacons.*

Ronald Rolheiser, in his book on eucharistic spirituality, makes the following claim:

> The Eucharist is not intended to be simply a ritual prayer within which we participate regularly, but is also meant to be something

that touches and colors every area of our lives. . . . We need
to be living and breathing the Eucharist all the time, not just
those times when we are in church. The Eucharist needs to be a
defining attitude, a way we meet life, receive it, and share it with
others. It needs to be a spirituality, namely, a way we undergo
the presence of God and others in this world.[12]

Rolheiser's claim makes it clear that our participation in the Eucharist comes to define all that we are as followers of Christ, all
that we do as deacons and priests of the Lord, and all that we offer
God's people as servant-leaders in the church.

To explore our "participation in" or "communion in" the body
and blood of Christ we will first look at some key principles regarding ordination and then at the nature of what happens in the
Eucharist and how it is inherently meant to transform those who
are its ordinary ministers. We will examine how the nature of God's
grace in ordination is continually at work in the ongoing process
of the transformation of a man of God into a deacon and priest
long after ordination. The Eucharist, as we will see, becomes the
privileged means of that grace of God transforming over time the
reality of the lives of ordained deacons and priests into living icons
of Jesus the servant and priest.

God Consecrates and Claims Us into On-going Conversion

The process of becoming a deacon in Christ, of becoming a
priest in Christ, is a slow process that takes most of our lives, not
merely before and during ordination, but throughout all the many
years after. Each of us can recall the moment when, at our ordination, we lay on the floor of a cathedral or church in an act of complete surrender to Christ. After the Litany of the Saints concluded
with a prayer by the bishop, we then knelt before the bishop in a

---

12. Ronald Rolheiser, *Our One Great Act of Fidelity: Waiting for Christ in the
Eucharist* (New York: Doubleday, 2011), 95.

humble posture of self-giving and of complete receptivity to the outpouring of the Holy Spirit. But when we rose from that floor and stood as a priest or a deacon, were we different persons? We were; but, at the same time, we were not.

We were, at the very core of our being, configured to Christ in a particular way for the people of God, but on the existential level, we were not any different. Emotionally, psychologically, cognitively, we were pretty much the same person we had always been. Our individual personalities did not change. The struggles and accomplishments, the moments of joy, and the times of anguish we experienced in life stayed a part of our personal history. All of our abilities and limitations still defined us. But God was not done with us.

Since our ordination calls us to a process of ongoing conversion and transformation, and since the Eucharist is central to our lives and ministry as ordained servant-leaders in the church, we then need to explore the connection between ongoing conversion/transformation and the continual celebration of the Eucharist. We will do this by exploring three key sacramental principles: the *ontological claim* by the Holy Spirit that happens within ordination, the *transformation* (what Bernard Lonergan calls "sublation") of the bread and wine into the body and blood of Christ, and the inherently eucharistic dimension of ordained ministry.

Before continuing with the rest of the book, in order that you might engage the material more on the level of a felt experience of entering into the eucharistic narrative, I suggest spending some time reflecting on what still needs to be claimed by the Holy Spirit within your own personal narrative. Then, you are encouraged to prayerfully acknowledge what still needs to be transformed within yourself and within the story of your life. These opportunities for "Prayer and Reflection" will be offered throughout the chapters of this book in order to encourage and foster a conscious interweaving of Jesus' eucharistic narrative with the personal story lines of the deacons and priests who read this text.

Prayer and Reflection

Take a few moments of silent reflection.
Prayerfully ponder the following:

What does the Holy Spirit still need to claim in you?
(What aspects of your personal story have you been
keeping off-limits to the sacramental grace of your
ordination?)

What still needs to be forgiven, transformed, healed,
strengthened, or ignited inside of you or in your life
or ministry?

chapter two

How the Holy Spirit Writes Our Narrative in Holy Orders and the Eucharist

And they all left him and fled.
　　　　—Mark 14:50

Observing the boldness of Peter and John and perceiving them to be uneducated, ordinary men, [the Sanhedrin was] amazed, and they recognized them as the companions of Jesus.
　　　　—Acts 4:13

Saul . . . was trying to destroy the church; entering house after house and dragging out men and women, he handed them over for imprisonment.
　　　　—Acts 8:3

I have been crucified with Christ; yet I live, no longer I, but Christ lives in me.
　　　　—Galatians 2:19-20

The Scriptures are filled with stories of the Holy Spirit effecting amazing transformations in individuals, including the amazing transformations of the first persons to say "yes" to Christ and emerge as servant-leaders in the church. Seemingly, the disciples and Saul—by this time well into adulthood—were thoroughly formed persons who were already set in their ways, with well-defined personalities and approaches to life. And so it is intriguing to inquire: What made the once frightened and cowardly apostles, who abandoned Jesus on the night he was arrested, so boldly different after Pentecost? What allowed the fiery Saul, who oversaw the martyrdom of Stephen and who formerly "[breathed] murderous threats" (Acts 9:1) against the earliest disciples of Christ, to profess that now he shared in the crucifixion of Christ who lived in him? To borrow from *Stranger Than Fiction*, we all know that the lives of the disciples had their own stories; but what if a larger story was really their lives?

When we look at ourselves, what allows a man, with an already established personality and ego-identity, to step forward to be ordained a deacon or priest, when all along he has been a broken human being, fraught with faults and failings? Has another story been writing his life? In a way, yes. It is nothing less than the narrative grace of the story of Jesus Christ. which is the transforming power of the Holy Spirit at work deep inside each person who professes faith in Jesus Christ and desires to serve him in the mission of the church. That narrative grace of the Holy Spirit, who so powerfully transformed the apostles, seeks to powerfully transform, through holy orders and the Eucharist, all ordained servant-leaders in the church.

The First Sacramental Principle: The *Ontological Claim* by the Holy Spirit

At our ordination, the Holy Spirit configured us to the diaconate and ministerial priesthood of Christ and brought about an essential and permanent oneness with Jesus the humble servant (deacon) and Jesus the eternal priest that was to be exercised for the sake of God's people. But while our diaconate and priesthood are those of Jesus Christ, the Son of God, they are also the diaconate and priesthood of the same Christ who became incarnate in order to touch, embrace, and heal every aspect of human brokenness. Therefore, the Holy Spirit, by configuring us to the Incarnate Deacon and the Incarnate Priest, claims everything about our humanness, including all that is broken about us as persons and as ordained men.

This is where there is a need perhaps to adjust some of our theological thinking in order to gain better spiritual insight. During the Middle Ages, the church, using the Greek philosophical category of *ontology* ("being"), taught that the three sacraments that are celebrated only once in the life of a believer—namely, baptism, confirmation, and holy orders—are unrepeatable because they affect the person on the ontological and not merely experiential and temporal levels. Very often, therefore, being ordained a deacon or priest was described by the church as an "ontological change"; and so it was, and still is.[1] However, as I have previously written:

> That kind of language all by itself without a wider sacramental context has proven to be problematic. In some cases it has led to clerical elitism and entitlement. In other cases it has led to ministerial malpractice and a lack of accountability since some priests [and deacons] mistakenly assumed that no matter how well or how poorly they perform their duties all will be satisfactory ordained ministry. And in some cases it has led to walking away from [diaconate or] priesthood because a man might never have experienced the benefits of ontological change in times of great loneliness or struggle.[2]

---

1. It is important to note that being baptized and confirmed must also be recognized as involving an ontological change, yet church tradition rarely spoke of this and almost exclusively reserved the phrase for ordination.

2. Scott Detisch, *From Hero to Servant to Mystic: Navigating the Deeper Waters of Priestly Spirituality* (Collegeville, MN: Liturgical Press, 2019), 54 (bracketed insertions added).

Because of these misconceptions, I have begun to speak less about *ontological change* and more about *ontological claim*. For me, this is a more fitting theological term that captures how, at our ordination, the Holy Spirit claimed us for the diaconate and priesthood of Jesus Christ at the very core of our being (hence, *ontologically*, as the church teaches) to be lived for the sake of God's people. However, the experiential effects of that claim will take the rest of our lives to unfold (hence, avoiding the word *change*, which suggests that what the Holy Spirit does in ordination is a finished endeavor or a completed act). The term *ontological claim* better captures how slowly over time our inner unity with Christ, effected by the Holy Spirit, needs to work its way through our personal identity and transform the very broken, limited, and flawed ways that we have lived out ordained ministry and experienced the diaconate and priestly life. This is what the Spirit claims by grace.

To be sure, the theological notion of the *ontological change* in a man who is ordained has tremendous value when it reminds us that priesthood and diaconate are not mere functions, jobs, or careers; nor are they the expressions of only a temporary commitment to Christ and his church in a man's life. Diaconate and priesthood are the manner in which the Holy Spirit unites a man's essence—personhood—and way of life to the identity of Christ as deacon or priest on behalf of the church and the world. However, it must be admitted that the experiential effects of this *ontological change* happen slowly over time, as the Holy Spirit draws the ordained man into deeper and more transformative encounters with grace.

Recall another moment from our ordination: it was the invocative prayer said for each one of us by the bishop after we pronounced our "I Do's" (for deacons and priests ordained in the 1990s or later) or our "I Am's" (for those ordained earlier). The ordaining bishop prayed: "May God who has begun the good work in you bring it to fulfillment." There is so much meaning and power in that invocation. Those words make it clear that, while our ordination came at the end of an extensive process of formation and training, it did *not* mark the end of our conversion.

It was not ritualizing any completion of our transformation nor was it solemnizing any conclusion of what God was trying to effect in us. God was only getting started! There was still so much inside of us that needed to be claimed and converted by the grace of God. There were still so many attitudes, forms of ignorance, types of blindness, and tepid styles of self-giving that needed to be transformed into the Way of Christ. There were still so many sinful inclinations, harsh memories, hurt feelings, and stubborn forms of resistance that needed to be healed by the power of the Holy Spirit that claimed us in a special way on the day of ordination.

The Second Sacramental Principle: The Eucharist as the Transforming Power of God in Diaconate and Priesthood

We are all familiar with St. Augustine's wonderful teaching on the Eucharist to newly initiated Christians. In one of his homilies, which we read in the Office of Readings during the Easter Season, Augustine says:

> If you wish to understand the body of Christ, listen to the Apostle [Paul] as he says to the faithful "You are the body of Christ, and his members (1 Cor 12:27). If, therefore, you are the body of Christ and His members, *your* mystery has been placed on the Lord's table; you receive *your* mystery. You reply "Amen" to that which you are, and by replying consent. For you hear "The Body of Christ," and you reply "Amen." Be a member of the body of Christ that your "Amen" may be true.[3]

When we are baptized into the body of Christ, our baptismal conformity to Christ is nourished and strengthened continually by the Eucharist. The Holy Spirit claims us for Christ in the waters of baptism, but our capacity to live Christ-like lives will need to

---

3. St. Augustine, "Sermon 272," in *The Eucharist*, Daniel J. Sheerin, The Message of the Fathers of the Church, vol. 7 (Wilmington, DE: Michael Glazier, 1986), 95 (emphasis added).

be nourished and strengthened for the rest of our lives. And this is what the Eucharist does.

Likewise, as ordained ministers of the Eucharist, the claim that the Holy Spirit has on us as deacons and priests is deepened and energized every time we celebrate the Eucharist. As the central element of our ministerial lives, the Eucharist is the "source and summit" of what it means for us to be ordained servants with and in Christ and ordained priests with and in Christ. Therefore, in the pages ahead a central theological principle within the doctrine of the Eucharist will be examined and then applied to ordained ministry that is centered on the Eucharist.

We all know that the Catholic Church has definitely taught for centuries that the Eucharist is the real presence of Christ. However, to be more exact, there are actually two elements in the doctrine of real presence. In its *Decree Concerning the Most Holy Sacrament of the Eucharist* (1551) the Council of Trent taught:

> The holy council teaches and openly and without qualification professes that, after the consecration of the bread and wine, our Lord Jesus Christ, true God and true man, is *truly, really, and substantially* contained in the propitious sacrament of the holy Eucharist under the appearance of those things which are perceptible to the senses.[4]

The Council follows with canon 1:

> If anyone denies that in the most holy sacrament of the Eucharist there are contained truly, really, substantially, the body and blood of our Lord Jesus Christ together with the soul and divinity, and therefore *the whole Christ . . .* let him be anathema.[5]

---

4. Session 13 of the Council of Trent, "Decree on the Most Holy Sacrament of the Eucharist," in *Decrees of the Ecumenical Councils*, vol. 2 (London: Sheed and Ward, 1990), 693 (emphasis added).

5. Council of Trent, "Decree on the Most Holy Sacrament," 697 (emphasis added).

The Council continues in its *Decree on the Eucharist*:

> But since Christ our Redeemer said that it was truly his own body which he was offering under the form of bread, therefore, there has always been complete conviction in the church of God . . . that, by the consecration of the bread and wine, there takes place the change of the whole substance of the bread into the substance of the body of Christ our Lord, and of the whole substance of the wine into the substance of his blood. And the holy catholic church has *suitably and properly* [most aptly] called this change transubstantiation.[6]

These citations demonstrate that the Council of Trent's teaching on the real presence of Christ in the Eucharist actually has two prongs to it. They are often called "eucharistic realism" and "eucharistic conversion." First, eucharistic realism is the doctrine that the bread and wine are the real presence of Christ—the *true, real,* and *substantial* presence of Christ. This means that *everything* of the personhood of Christ (body and soul, divinity and humanity) is present to us in the Eucharist. However, for this to be true, a second prong of the teaching is necessary—that the bread and wine are transformed, that is, converted into the real presence of Christ. The *Catechism of the Catholic Church* states:

> It is by conversion of the bread and wine into Christ's body and blood that Christ becomes present in this sacrament. The Church Fathers strongly affirmed the faith of the Church in the efficacy of the Word of Christ and of the action of the Holy Spirit to bring about this conversion.[7]

---

6. Council of Trent, "Decree on the Most Holy Sacrament," 695 (emphasis and additional translation added).

7. *Catechism of the Catholic Church*, 2nd ed. (United States Catholic Conference—Libreria Editrice Vaticana, 1997), 1375.

Thus, the doctrine of eucharistic conversion attests to the belief that if the bread and wine become the real presence of Christ, then they have to be radically and substantially transformed. They are no longer bread and wine. Their substance has changed into the substance of the body and blood of Christ; but their experiential qualities (what Aristotle called "accidents") remain the same. This is done by the power of the Holy Spirit and the words of institution from Christ.

The doctrine of eucharistic conversion has been labeled many different things over the last twenty centuries. Terms like *transfiguration, sanctification, transmutation,* among others, were used by church fathers for centuries. The Fourth Lateran Council (1215) was the first to use the term "transubstantiation." However, at the Council of Trent, because of the difficulties that the term *transubstantiation* (not the doctrine of eucharistic conversion) caused in fueling the flames of the Reformation, some bishops insisted that the decree read:

> And the holy catholic church has *suitably and properly* [*aptimisse appellat*—most aptly] called this change transubstantiation.[8]

They vetoed the attempts to say: "the church *exclusively* calls" or "the church *definitively* calls" this change transubstantiation.[9] The point is that the *doctrine* of eucharistic conversion is definitive; however, the *explanation* for how it occurs has changed over the centuries, depending on the philosophical categories of understanding that have been operative in any given era of church history. A more contemporary understanding of eucharistic conversion that will now be examined comes from Bernard Lonergan; it is his notion of *sublation.* It offers the clearest connection between (1) the power of the Holy Spirit to claim faith-filled men

---

8. "Decree on the Most Holy Sacrament of the Eucharist," c. 2, in *Decrees of the Ecumenical Councils*, 697 (emphasis and Latin text added).

9. See Edward Schillebeeckx, "Transubstantiation, Transfinalization, Transfiguration," *Worship* 40 (1966): 331.

and transform them into deacons and priests of Christ, and (2) the power of the Holy Spirit to claim bread and wine and transform them into the body and blood of Christ.

Lonergan described all true conversion as an ongoing process that involves all the different layers of one's personhood: intellectual, moral, and religious. Therefore, conversion is an integrated process that draws into it the psychological, emotional, intellectual, volitional (of the will), and spiritual dimensions of a person. Furthermore, conversion, for Lonergan, is a constantly repeated process of greater and deeper self-transcendence, in which the previous stages of thinking (intellectual), valuing (moral), and believing (religious) are not discarded, but instead are drawn into the greater depth of each subsequent stage.[10] The dynamic of sublation is key to this integrated conversion because, as Lonergan states, each further stage of self-transcendence "introduces something new and distinct, puts everything on a new basis, yet so far from interfering with the [previous] sublated [stage] or destroying it, on the contrary needs it, includes it, preserves all its proper features and properties, and carries them forward to a fuller realization within a richer context."[11]

Sublation, however, does not only capture the process of human conversion; it describes how anything can be converted from what it once was to what it now is. According to Lonergan, this is how sublation works: a lower order reality (or a lesser stage of growth and development) can be taken up to a higher order reality (or a higher, more advanced stage of growth and development) without the destruction of the lower order thing (or the previous stage). However, the higher order reality can no longer be identified or named as the lower order thing it once was; it has become sublated into the higher order thing without being annihilated.

Michael Stebbins, a noted analyst of Lonergan's thinking, cites the example of oxygen within a molecule of a red blood cell to

---

10. Bernard Lonergan, SJ, *Method in Theology* (Minneapolis: Seabury Press, 1972), 241.

11. Lonergan, 241.

demonstrate this point. He explains that a molecule of oxygen has its own identity as a real thing. However, once it becomes bonded to a molecule of hemoglobin it now becomes a part of a higher order thing—a red blood cell. It does not exist as itself, but also does not cease to have all the properties of oxygen. It brings all that it was into what it has become. Yet, since it has been assumed into a higher order thing, it can no longer be correctly identified simply as oxygen. The lower-order reality of oxygen has been sublated into the higher-order reality of a red blood cell.[12]

In applying this concept of sublation to the process of eucharistic conversion, Michael Stebbins explains that the lower-order realities of bread and wine become the higher-order realities of the body and blood of Christ without losing any of their qualities and characteristics as bread and wine. Stebbins contends that the eucharistic elements can no longer be identified as simply bread and wine, for they have become something infinitely more as the real presence of Christ. But they never lose anything of the experiential attributes of bread and wine. This is how Christ's body and blood become sacred food and drink for all of us.[13]

Sublation is basically the moving upward into a higher realm of existence those things that are of a lower level of reality; those things that are less complex in identity are lifted up into a more complex level. If this all sounds too philosophically intricate, think of the power of the resurrection to lift people up from death and from a more earthly existence into a more heavenly one. We see this principle described in the following passage from the Office of Readings (Fifth Sunday of Easter) in which St. Maximus of Turin writes:

> Christ is risen! He has burst open the gates of hell and let the
> dead go free; he has renewed the earth through the members of

---

12. J. Michael Stebbins, "The Eucharistic Presence of Christ: Mystery and Meaning," *Worship* 64 (1990): 225–36.
13. Stebbins, 228–30.

his Church now born again in baptism, and had made it blos-
som afresh with [people] brought back to life. His Holy Spirit
has unlocked the doors of heaven, which stand wide open to
receive those who rise up from the earth. Because of Christ's resurrection the thief ascends to paradise, the bodies of the blessed
enter the holy city, and the dead are restored to the company of
the living. *There is an upward movement in the whole of creation,
each element raising itself to something higher.*[14]

The effects of the resurrection are not merely on Christ nor only
for the dead; all of creation is taken up by the Holy Spirit here
and now into the higher level of grace that comes from Christ's
resurrection. This is the over-arching process of sublation within
salvation history.

Lonergan's principle of conversion as sublation can also be used
to explain how the Holy Spirit, who claimed us in ordination, is
constantly at work in us long afterwards. No matter how recently
or long ago we were ordained, the Holy Spirit is always seeking to
transform us from an earlier stage of personal, spiritual and ministerial development into a more developed stage, without losing
everything that we had previously been as very human men with
flawed personalities and personal histories, everything that made
us who we are from earlier periods of growth and development.
All of this the Holy Spirit draws into our self-surrender as men
giving ourselves to Christ in the diaconate and priesthood. In this
ongoing process, the repeated celebration of the Eucharist, which
lies at the center of our exercise of the diaconate and priesthood,
likewise plays a pivotal role in how the Holy Spirit sublates us more
and more into the deacons and priests we have been called to be.

14. A sermon from St. Maximus of Turin as quoted in "The Office of Readings" for Sunday, Week 5 of Easter, in *The Liturgy of the Hours: The Roman Rite*,
trans. International Committee on English in the Liturgy (New York: Catholic
Book Publishing, 1975), 815–16 (emphasis added).

While this concept of sublation might be new to us, we actually all agreed to it at our ordination. Recall the following words from the bishop during the ritual.[15] In eliciting the diaconal promises made by "the elect," the bishop asks:

> Do you resolve to *conform your way of life* always to the example of Christ, of whose Body and Blood you are ministers at the altar? (200)

In handing over the bread and wine to the newly ordained priest, the bishop instructs:

> Receive the oblation of the holy people, to be offered to God.
> Understand what you do, imitate what you celebrate,
> and *conform your life* to the mystery of the Lord's cross. (135)

What will be explored in the following chapters is how the Eucharist, which is inherently about the sublation of bread and wine into the body and blood of Christ by the power of the Holy Spirit, repeatedly draws ordained servant-leaders into that same power of the Holy Spirit.[16] In this way, the Spirit helps ordained deacons to conform their way of life into the example of Christ. Likewise, the sublating power of the Holy Spirit helps ordained priests to conform their lives into the mystery of the Lord's cross.

The fundamental conviction underlying this book is that, just as everything about bread and wine (their substance and proper-

---

15. *Rites of Ordination of a Bishop, of Priests, and of Deacons,* Second Typical Edition (2003), emphases added.

16. It is important to note that the Holy Spirit draws all the baptized into "sublating grace" through the Eucharist, not just those who are ordained. Since the focus of this book is on the spiritual lives of deacons and priests, the implications of this transformation on the people of God as a whole will not be explored in any depth. However, those implications for all the people of God can certainly be gleaned by what it said in this book about the eucharistic transformation of priests and deacons.

ties) is taken up by the Holy Spirit to become the body of Christ and the blood of Christ in the Eucharist, so too the Holy Spirit, through ordination and the Eucharist, takes everything about us ordained deacons and priests and transforms us into the real presence of Christ the servant and Christ the priest. Everything! Our identity, our personality, our relationships, our attitudes and emotions, our present and past, our abilities and our limitations, our knowledge and our ignorance, our joys and hopes, our grief and anxieties, our problems and pain, our successes and failures, our virtues and our vices. The Holy Spirit transforms our essence at ordination. But through the Eucharist, the Holy Spirit slowly over time transforms our personal history and our experiential qualities, drawing everything about us into higher and more developed levels of believing, living, ministering, making choices and decisions, and relating to Christ in prayer.

The Third Sacramental Principle: Ordained Ministry as Inherently Eucharistic

In the chapters that follow, we will look at the four main actions of the narrative of the Eucharist, which define our roles as deacons and priests within the Eucharist: we *take, bless, break,* and *give.* These four verbs come from the oldest accounts of the Eucharist. For instance, in Paul's First Letter to the Corinthians (11:23-26), we read:

> For I received from the Lord what I also handed on to you, that the Lord Jesus, on the night he was handed over, took bread, and, after he had given thanks, broke it and said, "This is my body that is for you. Do this in remembrance of me." In the same way also the cup, after supper, saying, "This cup is the new covenant in my blood. Do this, as often as you drink it, in remembrance of me." For as often as you eat this bread and drink the cup, you proclaim the death of the Lord until he comes.

Then, in the first gospel text of the Last Supper, found in Mark 14:22-23, we read:

> While they were eating, he took bread, said the blessing, broke it, and gave it to them, and said, "Take it; this is my body." Then he took a cup, gave thanks, and gave it to them, and they all drank from it. He said to them, "This is my blood of the covenant, which will be shed for many."

The four action words—take, bless, break, give—are often found together in the New Testament as indicative of a eucharistic meal. Many times, especially in the Synoptic Gospels, when Jesus is sharing a meal with his followers, we are told that he *took* bread, *gave thanks* (or *blessed* God), *broke* the bread, and then *gave* it to his followers to eat.

In these four actions, Jesus offers not only a pattern that we follow in the liturgy, he offers a pattern that we are to follow in our lives as his disciples, as his eucharistic people, and as his ordained deacons and priests. The four verbs form the plot sequence in the story that is to become our lives. In taking and blessing, Jesus demonstrates the fundamentally *receptive dimension* of our faith lives in which we, like Christ, take in and accept the goodness and bounty that God provides us through the stuff of our world and the very fabric of our lives. In breaking and giving, Jesus demonstrates the important *generative dimension* of our faith lives in which we, like Christ, uncover God's presence in all that we have been given, all that we experience, all that we encounter, and then we share in abundance the grace of God's presence with others. The spiritual movements captured by the eucharistic verbs can be summarized as follows:

TAKE: *to be attentive to what we receive*
> To "take" means to receive well the reality of our lives and to recognize the God-elements in all that we enjoy, all that we endure, all those we love, all those we struggle with, all that we succeed at, all that we fail at, all that we gain, and all that we

lose. To "take" entails a faith-filled *attentiveness* to the reality of ourselves and our lives, to the people we serve, to this current moment in the church, and to what is happening at this time in the larger world.

BLESS: *to be grateful in covenant with Christ*

To "bless" means that we recognize that everything in our lives is grace, and in seeing this we become filled with *gratitude* to God for all that God is for us and for all that God has been for us in the very stuff of our lives. When we bless, we discover the hidden presence of God in all of life and what that means for us. We see our lives as more than flawed human biographies; instead they are saturated with the loving presence of God and the mercy, wisdom, strength, and hope that God's presence always brings. To "bless" entails a bond with Christ who, at the Last Supper, defines blessing as entering into the covenant of his blood, which is the pulse of life and the self-emptying in death by which Christ blesses God.

BREAK: *to be in communion with the broken Christ as an offering to God*

Our attentiveness to the God-elements in all things and our gratitude for the grace of God in all things joins us intimately to the covenant of Christ and thereby allows us to find *communion* with Christ in our brokenness. To "break" is to enter into all that we are as broken human beings, where we discover a powerful oneness with the broken (crucified) Christ. This communion with the brokenness of Christ draws us into the self-giving of Christ to the Father on the cross, whereby Christ the eternal deacon and priest has consecrated all human brokenness as communion with him and the place of self-giving to the Father.

GIVE: *to be generative with and in Christ for the church*

Our communion with Christ in the breaking then empowers within us true *generativity* as men who are deacons and priests. In this generativity, we give our communion with Christ to the people of God whom we serve. To give means that we offer to others what God has made us with Christ and in Christ. What we have received from God has now become transformed into a gift for others. Our lives become truly generative in that we bring to life through our ministry all that God has been for us in the person of Jesus Christ.

It is important for us to consider how the liturgical roles of taking, blessing, breaking, and giving can be the very means by which the Holy Spirit effects more and more conversion in us.

We begin by looking at the nature of the liturgy of the Eucharist itself. In the *General Instruction of the Roman Missal* (72), we read:

> At the Last Supper Christ instituted the Paschal Sacrifice and banquet, by which the Sacrifice of the Cross is continuously made present in the Church whenever the Priest, representing Christ the Lord, carries out what the Lord himself did and handed over to his disciples to be done in his memory.
>
> For Christ took the bread and the chalice, gave thanks, broke the bread and gave it to his disciples, saying: Take, eat and drink: this is my Body; this is the chalice of my Blood. Do this in memory of me. Hence, the Church has arranged the entire celebration of the Liturgy of the Eucharist in parts corresponding to precisely these words and actions of Christ, namely:
>
> a) At the Preparation of the Gifts, bread and wine with water are brought to the altar, the same elements, that is to say, which Christ took into his hands.
>
> b) In the Eucharistic Prayer, thanks is given to God for the whole work of salvation, and the offerings become the Body and Blood of Christ.
>
> c) Through the fraction and through Communion, the faithful, though many, receive from the one bread the Lord's Body and from the one chalice the Lord's Blood in the same way that the Apostles received them from the hands of Christ himself.

This christological explanation of the meaning of the ritual deliberately defines the celebration of the Eucharist as a sacramental enactment of the actions of Christ in the midst of table fellowship with his disciples, most definitively during the Last Supper. Therefore, what we do in the Eucharist we are doing as persons configured to Christ. In other words, in and through us, it is *Christ* who takes, blesses, breaks, and gives during the celebration of the Eucharist.

But this fourfold action of Christ did not only happen during the final meal he shared with his disciples; it happened throughout his public ministry. Recall the moment in Matthew's gospel (14:13-21) when Jesus miraculously feeds a crowd. This takes place just after Jesus learns of the death of John the Baptist.

> When Jesus heard of it, he withdrew in a boat to a deserted place by himself. The crowds heard of this and followed him on foot from their towns. When he disembarked and saw the vast crowd, his heart was moved with pity for them, and he cured their sick. When it was evening, the disciples approached him and said, "This is a deserted place and it is already late; dismiss the crowds so that they can go to the villages and buy food for themselves." [Jesus] said to them, "There is no need for them to go away; give them some food yourselves." But they said to him, "Five loaves and two fish are all we have here." Then he said, "Bring them here to me," and he ordered the crowds to sit down on the grass. Taking the five loaves and the two fish, and looking up to heaven, he said the blessing, broke the loaves, and gave them to the disciples, who in turn gave them to the crowds. They all ate and were satisfied, and they picked up the fragments left over—twelve wicker baskets full. Those who ate were about five thousand men, not counting women and children.

Still later on, Jesus does the same thing again, with a smaller but still substantial crowd (Matt 15:32-38):

> Jesus summoned his disciples and said, "My heart is moved with pity for the crowd, for they have been with me now for three days and have nothing to eat. I do not want to send them

away hungry, for fear they may collapse on the way." The disciples said to him, "Where could we ever get enough bread in this deserted place to satisfy such a crowd?" Jesus said to them, "How many loaves do you have?" "Seven," they replied, "and a few fish." He ordered the crowd to sit down on the ground. Then he took the seven loaves and the fish, gave thanks, broke the loaves, and gave them to the disciples, who in turn gave them to the crowds. They all ate and were satisfied. They picked up the fragments left over—seven baskets full. Those who ate were four thousand men, not counting women and children.

When we look at all four Scripture passages in this section of the chapter, they cumulatively teach us three important things. (1) The central eucharistic actions define not only Jesus' final meal; they defined his whole life and ministry. (2) Jesus instructs his disciples to "do this in memory" of him. He also feeds the crowd *through* the disciples. All of this indicates that Jesus intends for his disciples (especially his disciples today who are priests and deacons) to be equally defined by the central actions of the Eucharist. For deacons and priests, this happens not only in the liturgical celebration of the sacrament, but in every ministerial and existential aspect of who we are as ordained disciples. (3) It is Christ who *takes*, *blesses*, *breaks*, and *gives* through our whole identity and ministry as deacons and priests. His story is our lives.

In essence, what the Holy Spirit does in the Eucharist *through* us as ordained ministers the Holy Spirit is also seeking to do *in* us by the Eucharist we celebrate. To summarize: through the celebration of the Eucharist, the Holy Spirit uses the narrative grace of the story of Christ to claim our own stories, that is, who we are, how we live, and what we do as consecrated servant-leaders in his church. In the personal narratives we brought to ordination, we may already have had well-defined personalities and we may already have been set in our ways, but the Holy Spirit gets to write the last word of our stories, and that word has not yet been written. The Holy Spirit is not done with us but still seeks to powerfully sublate the contents of our personal narrative into the eucharistic story of Jesus Christ.

Prayer and Reflection

Take a few moments of silent reflection.
Prayerfully ponder the following:

1. What have already been experiences in your life of being transformed by the grace of God?

2. Do you believe that God can effect more transformation in you or are you convinced that nothing much more about you can change?

3. What moments from the ordination ritual still have a hold on your self-awareness as a deacon or priest?

4. In what ways do you already sense a connection between what you do in ministry and what you celebrate in the Eucharist?

Part Two

The Eucharistic Narrative That Claims Deacons and Priests

chapter three

TAKE

For I received from the Lord what I also handed on to you.
—1 Corinthians 11:23

E very story has to begin somewhere. As noted in part 1, the eucharistic narrative of the person of Jesus Christ begins with the Son of God humbly emptying himself of glory and "taking" on human flesh, that is, the very real human condition. Similarly, the eucharistic narrative of the Lord's Supper begins with Jesus "taking" a loaf of bread and "taking" a cup of wine. Thus, our story begins with taking, which has different meanings and connotations. It is therefore important to get to the right sense of the verb in order to unlock its more profound eucharistic dimensions. First of all, "to take" can connote grabbing something greedily or wrongfully stealing from someone else, as in how a thief takes what does not belong to him, or when we are admonished not to take more than our fair share. Secondly, "to take" can convey the action of accepting something grudgingly, as in "I have to take my lumps for the mistakes I have made." But more deeply, the verb "take" can capture the capacity to receive something with gratitude or with equanimity because the one who takes is able to recognize what is meaningful and good in what is received. It is this meaning of the verb "take" that is most significant for us and that captures all the christological layers of what it means to take in order to bless, break, and give.

Taking as Receiving Our Own Lives

The initial action of taking implies that we graciously and gratefully receive what is given. Our taking occurs within a whole lineage of something being given, which is then received, and then subsequently offered to others. As St. Paul makes clear in his eucharistic instructions to the Corinthians, he is giving to them what he has received (taken) from the Lord. Paul makes it clear that the very context for the Eucharist originates within a faithful receiving of what the Lord has given. In the spiritual life, this receiving, or "taking," fundamentally means accepting with gratitude from our Creator the lives that have been handed to us, which means all that our lives have been, even the difficult struggles. It is the acceptance of our true personal narrative, which began with our parents giving us life as procreators with God. No matter what the circumstances were, our conception was God's first graced gift to us that we are to receive. This receiving of our lives (read: "taking graciously and gratefully") necessarily involves recognizing that everything that has happened to us has made us who were are and has brought us to this moment. Everything in our narratives has been part of the cauldron of life experiences that brought forth a man of faith who responded to a vocation to the diaconate or priesthood. More importantly, everything that has happened to us and all that has shaped us was claimed by God at our ordination because God consecrated our real selves for ministry, not a fictionalized, edited, whitewashed, or partial portrait of who we are and what has made us who we are.

When we "take," that is, receive, the lives that have been handed to us, we are admitting and accepting into our sense of self (as well as our sense of being an ordained man) all the particularities of our personal history. Each of our histories has involved a countless number of persons, some of whom were remarkably good individuals and others who were sources of great harm or pain, some of whom we were connected to in our lifetime, and some of whom came long before us but had an impact on the persons who influenced us. Furthermore, each of our personal histories has been defined by triumphs and tragedies, loves and losses, fulfilled dreams and dashed hopes, noble actions and sinful choices, amazing emotional highs and deeply painful lows. All of this is our true story, our real self.

As we receive the reality of our lives, at some point in our spiritual journey we then need to move away from two unhealthy and unproductive tendencies. The first is the shame-based need to either bury or rewrite the painful moments as if they did not happen. In the long run, this only fuels the shame even more because whatever gets buried or ignored will eventually push back with greater intensity and end up having an inordinate grip on our sense of self within our heart and inner spirit. The second tendency is when we become emotionally trapped in a fruitless desire to relive or reenact previous joyful experiences. Over time this causes us to spin in an endless cycle of regret over what our lives no longer are or what we no longer enjoy. Simply put: our lives are our lives. They are neither edited accounts of what really happened nor idealized depictions of what we have wanted them to be. They have been the true narratives of our real selves, that is, the narrative of our true incarnation as human persons who were created by God, have always been loved by God, and are now called and claimed by God for ordained ministry. Therefore, a habitual tendency not to "take" our true lives becomes a hardened propensity not to receive from God the real person he has made us to be, nor the true man God has called forth to be consecrated as a servant-leader in the church.

Time and again in working with seminarians, deacon candidates, deacons, or priests in either formation or spiritual direction, I have witnessed that, whenever a man keeps trying to avoid talking about some aspect of his life or some aspect of his personal identity, inevitably it surfaces in different ways. In some guys, there comes forth a very "contained" personality in which it seems that they are extremely measured in what they say among others and so very calculating in how they allow themselves to engage in life. In other men what comes forth is a very hostile, competitive, or aggressive pattern of dealing with other people, especially in situations of conflict or disagreement. Still others engage in addictive forms of compensatory behavior, from alcohol consumption to on-line addictions of gaming, pornography, or gambling. There are also those men who repeatedly draw people around them into patterns that satisfy the cleric's own unrequited emotional needs. Finally, in others, there is an inability to deal with the complexities of life, or to even notice them, for that matter. Until a man can receive his real life by acknowledging all the elements—good and bad—that have affected who he is, then he cannot yet take from the Lord the life he is called to live and he will not be able to "hand on" his life to be blessed, broken, and given for others as an ordained deacon or priest.

In receiving the lives that have been handed to us, it is important we keep in mind the true meaning of "taking" that is implied. First of all, by "taking" our lives we are not meant to become passive recipients of the pain in our lives or the unjust or harmful treatment from others that we may have endured. Nor are we meant to give into some fateful resignation that there is nothing to be done about the brokenness in our personal history. In other words, we are not called to "just take" what has been done to us or what has happened to us. Secondly, in receiving our lives we are not to "take hold" (as in "grab onto") only those people and events that brought us joy, pleasure, or fulfillment. We are not meant to confine our personal narrative only to some nostalgic remembrance of the positive things that we once experienced and now fondly recall. Eucharistic spirituality begins with the capacity to "take" what our lives have truly been and thereby receive in that taking the persons God has formed us to be through all the particularities that have defined us, both positively and negatively. Furthermore, before we "take" the bread and wine from God and God's people within the eucharistic liturgy, we need to "take" what God has been giving us in anything and everything we have experienced, since the God who entered into the broken sinful condition of humanity as Christ still enters into the broken, concrete conditions of our lives today.

As we will see in the next chapter, this is how we can then "bless" God with our lives, by recognizing how God has always somehow been graciously present to us in every chapter, every story line, and every episode of our personal narratives.

For those of you familiar with the writings of St. Ignatius of Loyola, this sounds a lot like his "Principle and Foundation," which undergirds his *Spiritual Exercises*.[1] The first element of St. Ignatius' "Principle and Foundation" (as well as the focus of the First Week of his exercises) calls for us to accept our creaturehood, which has been crafted by the hands of a loving and providential Creator. In short, God made us with love and so we are graciously to receive our lives, our humanness, our particularity as a gift of love from God. Yet we do this without blindness to the very real sinfulness

---

1. I find Timothy Gallagher's contemporary translation most helpful. It is as follows:

God created us out of love so that we might praise and reverence his infinite love and goodness, and by dedicating our lives to his service, might enter an eternity of joyful communion with him.

God created all the other things on the earth for us, to help us attain this purpose for which he created us.

As a result, we should appreciate and use these gifts of God—places, occupations, relationships, material possessions, and all the other blessings of God's creation—insofar as they help toward the purpose for which we are created, and we should let them go insofar as they hinder our attainment for this purpose.

Consequently, in choices in which we are free to choose among various options, we must hold ourselves as in a balance with regard to these gifts of God's creation. This means that for our part we do not set our desires on health rather than sickness, wealth rather than poverty, being held in honor rather than in little esteem, a long life rather than a short life, and likewise in all the rest.

Our only desire and choice is for what better leads us to the purpose for which God created us: to praise and serve him in this life, and so enter the joy of eternal life.

Found in Timothy Gallagher, *A Handbook for Spiritual Directors: An Ignatian Guide for Accompanying Discernment of God's Will* (Chestnut Ridge, NY: Crossroad Publishing, 2017), 153-54.

that has marked our lives, both our own sinfulness and that of others. We likewise acknowledge that our life story has had both grace-filled and gut-wrenching experiences, and this acknowledgement leads us to discover that in all of our experiences God has held us in love.

The second element of Ignatius' "Principle and Foundation" is that any concrete circumstance can be a means by which we love and serve the Lord. In other words, no matter what the particularities of our lives have been, now are, or will become, we can be blessed by God and bless God in return. Those particularities can be: health or illness, a loving family of origin or a rather broken one, a string of successes or a litany of failures, natural intelligence or difficulties in school, introversion or extroversion, vibrant friendships or a rather solitary life, a good marriage or a painful divorce, a long life or a short one. It is not that God causes any one of these; the point of receiving our particularity is to discover how God has been with us in what has unfolded in our lives. By "taking" our lives with the right spiritual depth, we sublate our lives from being merely an imperfect story of an imperfect human being to becoming a graced narrative of a man constantly loved by the God who has always been with him. This sublation calls for a prayerful examination of the content of our lives.

We have all heard the oft-quoted phrase attributed to Socrates (in Plato's *Apologia*) that "the unexamined life is not worth living." This adage is a summons to do more than just live life as a sequence of events which may or may not be enjoyable, may or may not bring fulfillment, or may or may not seem worthwhile. Instead, as rational creatures we are called to look critically upon the events and experiences of our lives to find the deeper meaning of what has been experienced in order to be more authentic and find more fulfillment and significance in what will be experienced. This is the examined life; and for all those who believe in God, such a life is crucial in allowing us to receive well the life we have been given, recognizing that it is saturated with the things of God which give one's life its true identity, value, and sense of purpose. Hence the examined life necessarily begins with a heightened capacity for awareness of the "God-element" in every moment, every person, every experience that constitute the narrative of a human life. While an underdeveloped but faith-filled awareness can reveal so much of the "God-element" in one's life, or at least assure one that God has been present in one's life, in order for priests and deacons to be more fully claimed by the Eucharist, a more heightened level of awareness is needed. This heightened awareness helps to make sure that the eucharistic stirrings of the Holy Spirit within a priest or deacon do not get stalled at the action of taking (as surely as the eucharistic liturgy does not end with the presentation of the gifts). In order for the taking to become blessing, a greater awareness in the form of a more intentional attentiveness is needed. This attentiveness is the habitual willingness to look deliberately and consciously for the presence and grace of God in all things in one's life, even long after the moments in which they occurred or were encountered. It is more than just recognizing in a generic or sporadic way that God has been in one's life; it is a focused, well-honed level of recognition of the particularity of God's grace in each particularity of one's life.[2]

For St. Ignatius of Loyola, this capacity for attentiveness happens through the daily *Examen*. This brief spiritual exercise is a prayerful recollection of one's day which is meant to heighten a person's awareness of (and gratitude for) the graces and blessings of God that were a part of the particular experiences within the course of that day. In addition, the *Examen* calls for a daily review of the moments when one's heart, mind, and spirit were drawn to the things of God and when they were drawn away from the stirrings of God.[3] Such prayerful attentiveness to our day ensures

---

2. The theological and spiritual implications of the notion of "particularity" (what John Duns Scotus calls *haecceitas*) will be addressed in the next section of this chapter.

3. For a good introduction to the practice of the *Examen,* read Timothy M. Gallagher, OMV, *The Examen Prayer: Ignatian Wisdom for Our Lives Today* (New York: Crossroads Publishing, 2006). For an explanation of the various ways of praying the *Examen* read Mark E. Thibodeaux, SJ, *Reimagining the Ignatian Examen: Fresh Ways to Pray from Your Day* (Chicago: Loyola Press, 2015).

that we receive our day well, that is, that we take each day with a heightened awareness of the God-elements of what occurred in our lives. This only happens when one develops a well-honed attentiveness to the things of God in every aspect of one's life—a faith-filled examination that recognizes that no matter what unfolded in any given moment, God was present and active in the moment as a source of grace.

In describing Ignatius' purpose for devising the daily *Examen*, Timothy Gallagher writes:

> For Ignatius . . . the consciously chosen remembrance of God's gifts is not just a moment in a spiritual day or simply a devout practice considered generally advisable and helpful. It is the *heart itself* of the way he understands God and relates to God. The *only* God he ever knew from the first moment of his conversion was this God who constantly bestows gifts of grace upon us, revealing through these gifts the infinite love with which we are loved.[4]

Thus, from Ignatius' perspective, the daily examined life leads to a deeper recognition of how the lives we have received (the lives we prayerfully and consciously "take") are saturated with the love and grace of God.

Without this recognition, it is difficult to receive the reality of our lives as they have truly been and accept ourselves as we truly are. Furthermore, if we cannot rightfully receive our lives, then we easily slip into resentments about the harsh moments as well as self-pity for every form of hurt or deprivation we endured. In addition, we easily succumb to envy of the lives of those who seem to be happier or who seemed to have had an easier and more enjoyable life; or we become afflicted with inordinate guilt and shame over our sinful behaviors or patterns. In short, we lose sight of how *God has been with us* throughout our whole narrative and within every element of our life's story.

---

4. Gallagher, *Examen Prayer*, 58.

"God-with-us" is the very name for the child of Mary, who is to be received by Joseph into his life. This is Emmanuel—*God-with-us-in-the-concreteness-of-our-lives.* Joseph and Mary are icons of the proper act of "taking" one's life as it really is (and not as one wants it to be), for they soon discover and experience that Emmanuel is received in the taking. Certainly, Joseph (the key figure in Matthew's account of how the pregnancy of Mary is revealed) was not planning on marrying a woman who had become pregnant by some strange means. Nor, most likely, did he plan to marry a woman who would remain a virgin throughout their marriage. Likewise, Joseph (and certainly Mary as well) would never have desired the difficult and treacherous circumstances in which the birth of his son unfolded, circumstances he was forced to navigate with nothing but his faith and trust in God to guide him. But Joseph discovered how God was with him in what he did not expect and did not prefer. In announcing 2021 as a Holy Year of St. Joseph, Pope Francis says of this remarkable man: "Joseph, then, teaches that faith in God includes believing that he can work even through our fears, our frailties, and our weaknesses. He also teaches us that amid the tempests of life, we must never be afraid to let the Lord steer our course."[5] Pope Francis later asserts: "In every situation, Joseph declared his own 'fiat,' like those of Mary at the Annunciation and Jesus in the Garden of Gethsemane."[6] In the end, it was Joseph's fiat to God, even in the unknown and unwanted situations that unfolded, which allowed him to receive the actuality of what was happening in his and Mary's narrative. This "receiving/taking," in turn, led to the birth of Christ, the Incarnation of God.

As the Incarnation of God, Jesus reveals that no matter what the particular elements of anyone's life story have been, God has been in that story the whole time—*not* as the cause of what happened,

5. Pope Francis, *Patris Corde,* Apostolic Letter on the 150th Anniversary of the Proclamation of Saint Joseph as Patron of the Universal Church (Vatican: Liberia Editrice Vaticana, December 8, 2020), part 2.

6. Pope Francis, *Patris Corde,* part 3.

but certainly as the companion in all that unfolded. As with Mary and Joseph, in receiving one's life, one receives Emmanuel. Experientially, this can happen in many different ways but it always means that each personal narrative can reveal God-with-us.

- For instance, it could mean that the son of an alcoholic parent can discover the inner sanctuary of God dwelling within him as an infinitely loving father and mother.

- It could mean that the man who was a star athlete growing up could discover that the confidence he gained through his athletic prowess is now meant to be the courage of Christ's Spirit to do the difficult things in ministry.

- It could mean that the one who felt safe and loved in his childhood can feel so wonderfully assured of God's love for him that now, as an adult, he is not afraid to recognize and deal with his own sinful patterns that need to change.

- It could mean that the adult man who, as a boy, often felt alone or an outsider, can experience an inner friendship with Christ that is now pivotal for his self-identity and self-acceptance.

- It could mean that the adult who never heard "I love you" or "I forgive you" as a child can become more earnest in hearing the inner voice of Christ who never stops speaking love and mercy to one's heart and soul.

- It could mean that the one who struggled in school or who failed to achieve certain goals in life can be led to a powerful humility that unites him deeply to the humility of Jesus so that God's grace, rather than the human ego, is more clearly evidenced in his life and ministry.

- It could mean that the man who experienced hurtful treatment, painful trauma, or heartbreaking loss early in life may come to discover later in life that all along God held onto him, that all along God was for him what he needed God to be.

- It could mean that the one who grew up in a very religious household or the man who came to faith later in his life discovers that his faith in God has made all the difference and has enabled him to become the true person he is called to be.

The list of particularities in any of our lives could go on and on. The point is that, no matter what the various and varying details have been in our personal narrative, the one constant has been Emmanuel—God-with-us-in-what-our-lives-have-really-been. Therefore, we need to "take" our lives and "receive" who God has always been for us. Again, this "taking" sublates our limited and often fractured human stories into a grace-filled narrative of God's companionship.

But what are the implications of this kind of "taking" for our spiritual and ministerial growth? First of all, it means that in our own prayer and reflection we need to review our life's story and gratefully receive our lives as God's greatest gift to us. Secondly, it means that our prayer and reflection ought to aid us in receiving who we really are—our true self. To try to gloss over or ignore what has been painful or what we regret, to try to focus only on what has been wonderful or what we have enjoyed, to try to distort what has really happened for whatever reason, is to be stuck in what spiritual writers call "the false self." We can never sustain the identity of being a deacon or priest if it continues to come from a false narrative of ourselves.

This spiritual acceptance of our true narrative comes with a caution stated earlier: We are not meant to view God as the cause of all the things that happened to us like some puppet master controlling all the details of our lives. It does mean that we receive rightly and we receive well our very specific life story as a revelation of Emmanuel. The necessary diaconal and priestly qualities of gratitude and self-giving (to be discussed in the following chapters) originate in the capacity to do this. If we are not truly attentive to how God has been with us in what actually has been the narrative of our lives, then we cannot cultivate a life of "giving thanks" (the original meaning of "Eucharist"), nor can we truly give ourselves to God's people in ministry. In his apostolic exhortation *Evangelii Gaudium*, Pope Francis says: "The joy of evangelizing arises from grateful remembrance; it is a grace which we constantly need to implore. . . . The believer is essentially 'one who remembers'" (13). And that remembrance needs to be filled with gratitude to God.

This remembrance (the eucharistic word *anamnesis*) comprises a third element in our spiritual and ministerial journey. As men who remember with gratitude what our lives have been, thereby receiving our lives as revelations of Emmanuel, we then recognize with deep faith that, no matter what we have experienced or gone through, God has never been absent; God has never been idle; God has never been silent. God has always been leading us to some grace that we were meant to receive. The diaconate and priesthood demand that we take what God gives us, what originates in God's self-giving, and not what we wish our lives have been or a fictitious life story we have created in our own minds. Otherwise, we become deacons and priests who offer God little in return and we become "false selves" disguised as men ordained for God's people.

Prayer and Reflection (Option A)

Take a few moments of silent reflection.
Prayerfully ponder the following:

1. Ask God for the grace of an open mind and a grateful heart.
   Ask Joseph and Mary to accompany you in this prayer.

2. Review at least one joyful experience from your personal life that surfaces in your memory.

- Try to remember as much detail as possible.
- Why does this experience stand out for you?

3. Ask God to reveal to you what God desires you to receive from that experience.
   - How was God present or active in the experience?
   - What insight(s) are you receiving? (Keep in mind that true insight does not have to be earth-shattering. At times it can be subtle and uncomplicated.)
   - If you want, write down your insight(s) for further reflection.

4. Later repeat the same exercise with a difficult experience from your personal life.

Prayer and Reflection (Option B)

Take a few moments of silent reflection.
Prayerfully ponder the following:

1. Ask God for the grace of an open mind and a grateful heart.
   Ask Joseph and Mary to accompany you in this prayer.

2. Consider the particularities of your personal life right now (relationships, health, sense of well-being and fulfillment, joys, difficulties, recent successes and failures, etc.).

3. What are the ways you can discern that God has been with you through these particularities, especially the ones that come to your mind more strongly?

Repeat this exercise with the particularities of your place of pastoral assignment.

Taking as Receiving This Moment in the Life of the Church

All that was discussed in the previous section on what we do spiritually with our own personal narratives, we are also to do with the narrative of the church as it has unfolded in our lives and as it is now in this moment of history. You and I are deacons and priests in a time that has followed excruciatingly painful revelations of clergy abuse in the church. Furthermore, many of us are ministering within local churches that are experiencing tremendous decline in population and resources. This has caused a significant decrease in baptisms, first communions, confirmations, weddings, and vocations. In addition, we are part of a much larger church in great transition (which it always is) that presents its own unique challenges and opportunities. For instance, we are increasingly seeing people exit the church for many different reasons.

In their document *Disciples Called to Witness: The New Evangelization,* the US bishops note the following about our current situation:

Today, through the ministry of the Church, Jesus continues to call all people to himself. It is estimated that only 23 percent of US Catholics attend Mass each week. Those 77 percent absent from the eucharistic feast each week are not strangers: they are our parents, siblings, spouses, children, and friends. According to a recent Center for Applied Research in the Apostolate (CARA) study, the most common reasons given by Catholics who do not regularly attend Mass are not related to controversial issues. The reasons given instead point to a gradual slipping away from the faith. Most Catholics stop attending Mass because they (1) have busy schedules or a lack of time, (2) have family responsibilities, (3) have health problems or disabilities, (4) have conflicts with work, (5) do not believe missing Mass is a sin, or (6) believe that they are not very religious people. In other words, many of our brothers and sisters have simply drifted away from the Church. This is due in part to the busyness of modern life and to a changing culture. There are also Catholics who attend Mass on a regular basis but who feel unconnected to the parish community. The reasons for not attending Mass highlighted in CARA's study also point to an increased secularization, materialism, and individualism.[7]

In trying to address the causes of this difficult portrait of the current narrative within the church in the United States, the bishops offer the following analysis:

> Secularism influences all aspects of society, claiming religion is merely a private matter. Pope Benedict XVI has cautioned, "Any tendency to treat religion as a private matter must be resisted. Only when their faith permeates every aspect of their lives do Christians become truly open to the transforming power of the Gospel." Materialism also presents an obstacle to Christ. The ability to acquire limitless goods and an overreliance on science create a false sense of hope that we alone can fulfill our deepest needs. However, without God, our deepest needs

---

7. United States Conference of Catholic Bishops, *Disciples Called to Witness: The New Evangelization* (2012), part 1, http://usccb.org/beliefs-and-teachings /how-we-teach/new-evangelization/disciples-called-to-witness/upload/Disciples -Called-to-Witness-5-30-12.pdf.

cannot be fulfilled. "Without God, who alone bestows upon us what we by ourselves cannot attain (cf. *Spe Salvi*, 31), our lives are ultimately empty. People need to be constantly reminded to cultivate a relationship with him who came that we might have life in abundance (cf. n10:10)." Individualism leads to harmful forms of freedom and autonomy. After all, "we were created as social beings who find fulfillment only in love—for God and for our neighbor." Our personal relationship with Christ does not hinder our participation in the community of believers— the Church. In addition, there is an unsettling ignorance of the Eucharist as well as an erosion of Sunday as the Lord's Day dedicated to prayer and rest. The reasons that Catholics cite for missing Mass can be met and overcome by parishes that foster a welcoming environment for adolescents, young adults, singles, married couples, parents, families, the sick or disabled, and anyone who is no longer active in the faith. The means for fostering a welcoming environment is the New Evangelization. The New Evangelization places a special emphasis on welcoming back to the Lord's Table all those who are absent, because they are greatly missed and needed to build up the Body of Christ. (*Disciples Called to Witness*, part 1)

What all of this suggests is that you and I are deacons and priests in a very broken church. By the way, we have always been a broken church; the only difference now is that we are admitting this out loud because we cannot do otherwise anymore. But we are also deacons and priests in a moment in which the church needs so much from us in order to engage people through evangelization. While demographically many of our local churches are no longer the size they once were (many are much smaller; others are seeing significant growth), we are being challenged to become the church we had never been but now are called to be—a church of the New Evangelization filled with "missionary disciples," as Pope Francis says. Today we are a church that is thinking and planning in terms we never have before. This is the true, real "now" in our lived experience as a church. It is the actual narrative that defines our particular moment in the church.

John Duns Scotus, the 13th-century Franciscan philosopher, captured well an important theological principle that can be aptly applied to how we are to receive the church that has now been handed on to us: the notion of *haecceitas*, which recognizes that the sacred is encountered in the particularity or "this-ness" of our experiences.[8] The notion of *haecceitas* invites us to discover our intimacy with Christ in the particularities of our lives. This manner of spiritual exercise allows us to cry out in certain belief, "Christ is with me in *this* experience." We can assert with confidence, "Christ is here with me in *this* painful or unsettling or difficult time in my life." As a church we can say, "Christ is with us right now in this moment of the church, in this diocese, in this parish." In short, Christ is our companion in *this* moment, whatever *this* moment may be. In every "this-ness" God is with us.

From such a perspective, then, we are called to take this very moment in the church in which we find ourselves and receive it as a revelation of Emmanuel. Yet, this evokes a series of very difficult questions: How has God been with us even in the midst of the darkness of the abuse crisis, with the loss of any veneer that the clerical state is a higher state of holiness and virtue? How is God with those in holy orders as we struggle to make sense of how some in holy orders have been vile predators of the young? How is God with any local parish or diocese that no longer has the number of people in the pews or the number of baptisms, first communions and confirmations that it once did? How is God with those dioceses that have had to combine or close parishes and has had far fewer ordinations that it once had? How is God with the parishes that have growing numbers of members, especially among immigrant populations, but insufficient resources to meet

---

8. See John Duns Scotus, *Early Oxford Lecture on Individuation,* trans. Allan B. Wolter (St. Bonaventure, NY: Franciscan Institute, 2005), especially 81–85.

their needs? How are we to receive this moment that calls for us to be much, much better at evangelization and preaching than we ever had to be before? How are we to take the challenge from Pope Francis that we have to be *missionary* disciples if we are going to be *authentic* disciples at this moment in time? How are we going to take the signs of the times that call us as priests and deacons to become skilled at something (for example, evangelization) we might never have really been trained to do?

The simple but obvious answer is: *we take it into our prayer*, including our daily *Examen*. We are called to take this very moment in the church—the church as it now is and not once was; the church we experience right now and not merely the church we hope it can be—and we ask God to reveal to us the grace he is offering us in this moment. If we fail to or refuse to *take* and *graciously receive* all that God has brought into our lives and into our church, including in the present moment, then we are defying the very Eucharist we celebrate. If we fail or refuse to *take* and *gratefully receive* the abundant grace that God has always provided in every experience of our lives and every moment in the church, then our own lives and ministry will not offer to others the fruits of the Eucharist we celebrate. However, when we rightfully take this moment in the church into our prayer then we allow it to be sublated from a difficult moment in history into an encounter with God in the "this-ness" of our church as a whole, the "this-ness" of our diocese and parish, the "this-ness" of this period of ordained ministry.

Taking our "this-ness" into prayer does not always lead to solutions for problems, relief from difficulties, a change in the circumstances, nor sudden insight into what needs to happen. While these results can certainly come from prayer, the eucharistic receiving of our *haecceitas* is more along the lines of pondering our particularities and holding them inside of us in a way that comes from our intimate connection to Christ. Mary is the model of such pondering. In Luke's infancy narrative, Mary is often depicted as one who ponders. She wonders about the meaning of Gabriel's greeting toward her (Luke 1:29). In her heart Mary reflects on all the strange circumstances of her son's birth, including the significance of the shepherds coming to visit her newborn son and relay the message of the angels (Luke 2:19). Along with her husband Joseph, she is amazed at what Simeon says of their son at his presentation in the temple (Luke 2:33). Finally, after the difficult but revealing experience of her lost adolescent son being found in the temple sitting amongst the teachers of Judaism, Mary "kept all these things in her heart" (Luke 2:51).

In addition, John's gospel depicts the paradigmatic moment of Mary's pondering as she stands at the foot of the cross beholding her crucified son, unable to do anything to stop it (John 19:25). Yet, Mary's pondering is powerful. Ronald Rolheiser invites us to reflect on the image of Mary at the foot of the cross:

> On the surface it appears that she is doing nothing at all. She does not speak, does not try to stop the crucifixion, and does not even protest its unfairness or plead Jesus' innocence. She is mute, seemingly passive, not overtly doing anything. But on a deeper level she is doing all that can be done when one is standing under the weight of the cross, she is holding and carrying the tension, standing in strength, refusing to give back in kind, and resisting in a deep way.[9]

After describing the nature of Mary's standing by her crucified son in silence, Rolheiser goes on to state: "What Mary was doing under the cross, her silence and seeming unwillingness to protest notwithstanding, was radiating all that is antithetical to crucifixion: gentleness, understanding, forgiveness, peace, light, and courage."[10]

There was a lot going on in Mary's pondering. And it was sheer grace, because Mary was receiving all the particularities of her life—the perplexing messages and circumstances, the joyful events,

9. Ronald Rolheiser, *Sacred Fire: A Vision for a Deeper Human and Christian Maturity* (New York: Image Books, 2014), 147.

10. Rolheiser, 148.

and the excruciatingly painful moments—into the deepest place inside herself where she was always intimately connected to God's loving presence. It is from that deep place that Mary discerned what to do about the particularities that were part of her sacred narrative. Her pondering allowed her to know when to speak and when to be silent, when to act and when to stand in place, when to make decisive changes and when to accept what could not be changed. Mary took what her life really was and found intimacy with God in all of it. In the manner of St. Paul's words to the Corinthians quoted at the beginning of this chapter, what Mary has taken and received, she has handed on to all of us.

Like Mary, we too are to take into the deepest place in ourselves the particularities of our personal lives, the particularities of this present moment in our church as a whole, and the realities of our particular parish or place of ministry. Like Mary, we are to ponder our *haecceitas* in a way that holds it within a place of intimacy with Christ so that, like Mary, we too can discern when we are to act decisively in order to make things better or meet the needs of changing circumstances, but also when we need to accept things as they are. Our pondering will help us know when we are to speak up and speak out, but also when we need to be silent so that something else from God can come to the fore. Our prayerful receiving of our "this-ness" allows whatever "this" is to be a moment and a place where the grace of God is revealed. As we will see in the next chapter, this essential element of receiving all the particularities within this moment of our lives and our church allows our "taking" to become "blessing" in our eucharistic narrative. Without such pondering, our capacity as deacons and priests to hand on to our people the grace of God we have received becomes anemic and feeble.

Prayer and Reflection

Take a few moments of silent reflection.
Prayerfully ponder the following:

1. God, I know/knew some of the people on the list of
   accused abusers.
   - What am I supposed to do with the unbelievable
     anguish this has caused me?
   - How are you with me, God, in the agony and
     shame I feel over the painful revelations of abuse
     in the church?
   - What are you trying to say to me in this moment?
   - What do you desire to be for me in this moment?

2. God, I grew up in a vibrant parish with lots of people
   in the pews and so much activity going on day after
   day. My first assignments exhibited growth and vitality in the parish. But now I see so many empty
   spaces before me at Mass. I celebrate far more deaths
   and burials than baptisms and weddings. Despite
   our best efforts, we never see our young people after
   confirmation and they so often move away, taking
   all of their gifts and talents with them.
   - How is the energy of your Holy Spirit operating
     within all of this?
   - What is your grace providing in the midst of what
     my parish really is right now?
   - What are the signs of your Son's living presence
     in the particular circumstances of the parish at
     this moment in time?

3. God, I never even heard the word evangelization
   when I was growing up or even when I was being
   trained to be a deacon or priest. It might have been

mentioned a few times, but it was certainly never emphasized. Now all I am hearing about is the New Evangelization and that we are all called to be evangelizers. I'm not even sure I know what that means.

- Since clearly this a sign of the times in the church, how is your Holy Spirit trying to help me with this task?
- How is your Spirit helping me with my reluctance or fear, my ignorance or confusion, about being an evangelizer?
- How are you with me in trying to reach people that I have not reached before with my preaching and ministry?
- Can your grace ever stir inside of me as excitement and enthusiasm for the tasks needed right now in the church?
- Can your grace now help me to see diaconate or priesthood as missionary diaconate or missionary priesthood, no matter how long or how recently I may have been ordained?

Spend some time in silence so that God can answer whichever questions God wants to answer at this time.

Taking as Receiving the Gifts of the People of God

The spiritual narrative of the Eucharist within the life of a deacon or priest does not begin only with taking and receiving into our pondering all the circumstances and elements of life outside of the eucharistic ritual. Within the sacred liturgy itself, the act of taking constitutes the central gesture of the deacon and priest as they receive the bread and wine from the people. There is so much depth of meaning in that simple yet profound act. First of all, it is important to note what the *General Instruction of the Roman Missal* prescribes:

> It is a praiseworthy practice for the bread and wine to be presented by the faithful. They are then accepted at an appropriate place by the Priest or the Deacon to be carried to the altar. Even though the faithful no longer bring from their own possessions the bread and wine intended for the liturgy as was once the case, nevertheless the rite of carrying up the offerings still keeps its spiritual efficacy and significance. (73)

In the ancient church, the bread was made by the faithful in their homes and the wine came from their personal storerooms. Thus, there was a clear and demonstrative link between the eucharistic elements and the daily lives of the eucharistic people. The "spiritual efficacy and significance" of the faithful presenting the bread and wine continues today when we consciously recognize in the act of presenting the bread and wine the self-offering of the lives of our faithful people with all of their particularities. In handing on to a priest or deacon the bread and wine (along with their monetary contributions), the people of God are handing on their very selves to the Lord. In doing so, the liturgical act of a deacon and priest taking bread and wine from worshipers becomes sublated into a receiving of the self-sacrifice and self-offering of the people of God. We receive their *haecceitas* that is intimately joined to their faith in Christ.

This leads to the second important layer of this ritual of the presentation of the gifts. Within the very brief moment that is needed for us as a deacon or priest to take the bread and wine from the people and bring those gifts to the altar, we need to let their offerings pass through our hearts. We need to receive into ourselves the very real lives of our faithful people that are symbolized by the gifts of the bread and wine. The individuals bringing forward the bread and wine represent all of our parishioners, whether they are in our worship space at the moment or not. The faithful presenters of the gifts are presenting all the faithful self-sacrifices made by parents for their children, teachers for their students, coaches and mentors for those in their charge. The gift-bearers are bringing forth all the moments of joy and celebration that have happened in the lives of parishioners in recent days and weeks; they are also bearing all the sorrow and anguish that have occurred as well. Within the presented bread and wine is so much: every moment a parishioner sat by the bedside of a dying spouse or aging parent or afflicted child; every moment a parishioner reached out to someone in need; every instance when a faithful member of the community sought forgiveness from another or extended it to another; every moment someone collapsed in tears and despair as well as every time someone was brought to laughter and joy. Everything of the real "stuff" of the real narratives of our faithful people's lives is being brought forward in order to be taken—to be received—by the deacon and priest.

Thirdly, in receiving the real narratives of our people's lives we are also graciously and gratefully receiving our parish or faith community. As with our own personal lives, we are to take our parish as it truly is without editing, whitewashing, idealizing, or compartmentalizing the particularities that define our community of faith as "this" community. We receive "this" local portion of the people of God as the particular community for whom we are a deacon or priest, a community that most assuredly does some things very well but most definitely struggles with other aspects of what it means to be the church. To be sure, our particular community has remarkable saints sitting in the pews right next to notable personalities who are often difficult and demanding. The "this-ness" of our faith community includes its particular history, with all of its accomplishments, all of its plans for the future, and all of the residue of its past struggles. It includes the physical structures the community has built for worship and sacraments, faith formation, meetings and social gatherings, which may be in fine condition or may need a lot of work. Moreover, let us not forget that the real narrative of our faith community includes the very real volunteers and paid staff members, each of whom brings particular gifts, abilities, and shortcomings. In the end, what we receive within the bread and wine is the true, real, unfiltered narrative of our faith community as it really is. And we take it into our hearts as we take the bread and wine to the altar.

Think about what this means; the few brief steps to the altar from the place where, as deacon or priest, we take the bread and wine from the gift-bearers are to be the paces of pondering (but not the only time for pondering). We are to allow our procession to the eucharistic table with bread and wine in hand, as brief as it may be, to be a powerful moment, when we carry in our hearts and we hold with the Lord all that has been in the lives of the people we serve.

Finally, the spiritual nature of our "taking" consists in receiving our people and our parish as gifts from God. Just as we need to do with our personal lives, we need to receive the lives of our people and the life of our faith community with deliberate recognition that God is received within the "taking." Like the bread and wine being placed on the altar, our people and our parish are fruits of God's creation and the products of human effort. In what they strived for and what they have failed at, God has been with them. In their joy and hope as well as grief and anxiety, Emmanuel was there. In all that manifests their holiness and all that gives evidence to their brokenness, God has never been apart from them. And God comes to us in them; therefore, in taking them into our own hearts as we take their gifts to the altar, we are receiving all that God has been for them, with them, and in them.

Prayer and Reflection

Take a few moments of silent reflection.
Prayerfully ponder the following:

1. Who are the people whose faces you most recall as you hold a mental image of your eucharistic community? How do they convey something of God's presence to you?

2. Offer a prayer of gratitude to God for them.

3. What are the struggles and joys going on in your parish or faith community at this time? Bring all this to God.

4. Who are some of the people going through a very difficult or very painful time right now? Who is dying or caring for a dying loved one? Commend them to God's love and mercy.

5. What are some of the joyful moments and celebrations that people have recently experienced in their personal lives? (Marriages, new births, graduations, receiving of sacraments, job promotions, exciting travel experiences, recovery from a serious illness or injury, etc.)

Offer a prayer of thanksgiving to God on their behalf.

chapter four

BLESS

Blessed are you, Lord God of all creation,
for through your goodness we have received
the bread we offer you . . .
. . . the wine we offer you . . .

— The Roman Missal

Only after we have properly taken can we then rightfully "bless." This is the only way our eucharistic narrative can move to the next chapter. However, just as with the verb "to take," there are so many different ways of understanding what it means "to bless." Certain connotations of the word properly open up the eucharistic layers of how we bless what we have taken. Commonly, we think that God is the one who blesses. We invoke God to bless persons, places, food, endeavors, events, sacred or beloved objects, etc. In the same vein, deacons or priests might offer a blessing in the name of God at a parish gathering, meal, or sacramental moment. In this line of thinking, many would naturally assume that, within the context of the Eucharist, the verb "bless" connotes the Catholic sense of God "consecrating" the bread and wine. That is certainly a valid perspective, for indeed, by the invocation of the Holy Spirit and Christ's words of institution spoken by the priest, the bread and wine are consecrated into the body and blood of Christ. Admittedly, the *General Instruction of the Roman Missal,* when explaining the meaning of the *epiclesis* and *the institution narrative and consecration,* expresses this perspective.[1] Nevertheless, that connotation all by itself leaves out the scriptural meanings of blessing that lie deep within the eucharistic meal. Prior to its explanation of the chief elements of the eucharistic prayer, the *GIRM* has this to say about the meaning of the eucharistic prayer:

> Now the center and summit of the entire celebration begins; namely, the Eucharistic Prayer, that is, the prayer of thanksgiving and sanctification. The priest invites the people to lift up their hearts to the Lord in prayer and thanksgiving; he unites the congregation with himself in the prayer that he addresses in the name of the entire community to God the Father through Jesus Christ in the Holy Spirit. (78)

Prior to the "descending" movement of God consecrating the eucharistic elements and sanctifying the people through them there is first the "ascending" movement of the hearts of the eucharistic assembly in thanksgiving and praise to God. In other words, before God further "blesses" the bread, the wine, and all of us (through the eucharistic elements), we first "bless" God by our giving thanks and praise to him. However, our blessing of God is a response to the way God has already blessed all that makes up the lives we have received with his abiding love and grace. This is the deeply biblical and ancient notion of the verb "to bless" that lies within the story of Jesus which becomes our story.

In the Jewish world of meaning from which Jesus arose, all meals are sacred; and at every meal the participants turn to God. However, they do not ask God to bless the food; instead, the participants bless God for the gifts of food that come from the land that God has created and given to them. In the Deuteronomic reform of Judaism, a result of the Babylonian exile in the sixth

---

1. See *GIRM,* 79 c and d.

century BCE, there began the custom of the Jewish ritual meal. The need for this ritual meal originates in the writing of the Book of Deuteronomy which occurred at this time. The book recounts how Moses, as he ratifies the covenant with God in the midst of the chosen people, instructs them:

> For the LORD, your God, is bringing you into a good country, a land with streams of water, with springs and fountains welling up in the hills and valleys, a land of wheat and barley, of vines and fig trees and pomegranates, of olive trees and of honey, a land where you will always have bread and where you will lack nothing, a land whose stones contain iron and in whose hills you can mine copper. But when you have eaten and are satisfied, you must bless the LORD, your God, for the good land he has given you. Be careful not to forget the LORD, your God, by failing to keep his commandments and ordinances and statutes which I enjoin on you today. (Deut 8:7-11)

Eventually, Jewish religious tradition interpreted Moses' instructions as a mandate to end each meal with a prayer of thanksgiving to God for the bounty of the land. This prayer evolved into the *Birkat ha-Mazon*. Whenever there is a meal, this prayer is said. While there was never a formalized text of the *Birkat ha-Mazon* (especially since there was a prohibition against putting the prayer in writing), it did follow a certain pattern:

> Blessed are you, Lord, our God, king of the universe, who feed the whole world in goodness, kindness, and mercy.
> Blessed are you, Lord, who feed the universe.
>
> We thank you, Lord, our God, who have given us as an inheritance a desirable land, that we might eat of its fruits and nourish ourselves on its goodness.
> Blessed are you, Lord, our God, for the land and the food.

Have mercy, Lord, our God, on Israel your people and on Jerusalem your city and on Zion the dwelling place of your glory and on your altar and sanctuary.

Blessed are you, Lord, who build Jerusalem.[2]

The *Birkat ha-Mazon* tells the meaning of the meal in Judaism and discloses how God is blessed. As a fundamental starting place, the ancient devout Jews recognized that the land was given to them by the Lord as a pledge of the covenant. Therefore, to eat the produce of the land was an acceptance of this covenant. Thus, in every meal devout Jews blessed God, first of all, by giving praise and thanks to God for the land and the food and, secondly, by renewing their assent to live the terms of the covenant with God. As a devout Jew, Jesus naturally connected the sharing of a meal with blessing God and renewing the covenant with God. With that in mind, it is important to note that, whether the Last Supper was a Passover meal (Synoptics) or a preparation for Passover (John), either way the *Birkat ha-Mazon* would have informed Jesus' actions when he was at table with his disciples; however, the terms of the covenant are now defined by the self-giving of Christ in his life and in his death.

Mark's account of the Lord's Supper, quoted earlier in chapter 2, shows the interconnection between the Jewish understanding of blessing God and giving thanks to God that lies deep within the Lord's Supper. Recall how Mark writes: "While they were eating, [Jesus] took bread, *said the blessing*, broke it, and gave it to them, and said, 'Take it; this is my body.'" Then he took a cup, *gave thanks*, and gave it to them, and they all drank from it. He said to them, 'This is my blood of the covenant, which will be shed for many.'"[3] For the most part, Matthew significantly repeats Mark's version with the important addition of the notion that Jesus' blood of the covenant is "shed on behalf of many for the forgiveness of

---

2. A proposed text by L. Finkelstein in "The Birkat ha-mazon," *Jewish Quarterly Review*, n.s., 19 (1928–29): 211–62.
3. Mark 14:22-24 (emphasis added).

sins" (Matt 26:28). Luke goes so far as to indicate that in the cup of Jesus' blood is "the new covenant" (Luke 22:20).

These scriptural accounts of the eucharistic actions of Christ indicate that after the bread and wine have been taken by the Lord, he then blesses and thanks God for being the source of what has been received. Therefore, the eucharistic action of taking, which is constituted by a profound awareness of the God-dimension of what has been received, is to awaken a deep sense of gratitude for what God has been offering all along in what has been received. Thus, the eucharistic action of taking grows into the eucharistic impulse for blessing God in the following way: (1) the process begins by developing a faith-filled attentiveness to how God has been present within what we have received and what God has done to bring about what we have taken (see previous chapter); (2) it continues as profound gratitude for what God offers us in what has been received and a desire to express that gratitude to God; and (3) this gratitude becomes the renewal of our assent to participate in covenantal life with God, yet now in new terms, for to eat and drink this meal is to eat and drink the covenant that is embodied in Christ. Thus blessing God essentially expresses gratitude to God, which then leads to assent to live the covenant with God as defined by the life and death of Christ.

When this act of blessing truly claims the life of a deacon or priest, that life is sublated from being merely the personal narrative of a human being to being the story of an ordained man whose heart, mind, and will are configured to Christ. The sacred story of Jesus becomes the life of the deacon or priest. More specifically, the deacon or priest, who has rightfully received his life from God, now allows that life to be transformed into Christ's complete self-giving to the Father on the cross for the sake of all of God's people. One's *personal* narrative now becomes the *paschal* narrative. In other words, the life we have received *from* God is now sublated into Jesus' very own self-offering *to* God. In this sublation of our lives, God is blessed. Let us now look at two important dimensions of the action of "blessing" in the Eucharist, namely, gratitude and assent.

Blessing as Profound Gratitude for What God Has Given

The poet David Whyte captures well the deeper dimensions of gratitude as he seeks to define the word more profoundly. He writes:

> Gratitude is not a passive response to something we have been given, gratitude arises from paying attention, from being awake in the presence of everything that lives within and without us. Gratitude is not necessarily something that is shown after the event, it is the deep *a priori* state of attention that shows we understand and are equal to the gifted nature of life.[4]

Understanding the true nature of gratitude captures well the inherent movement from "taking" to "blessing." When that "taking" comes out of a keen attentiveness to the God-dimension in all that is received, it leads one's mind, heart, and inner spirit to a desire to "bless" God with gratitude.

The Liturgy of the Hours prayed daily by deacons and priests is filled with psalms and canticles that connect blessing God with praise for God's mighty deeds and with gratitude for what God has done. For instance, in the Canticle of the Three Young Men that we often recite at Morning Prayer on Sundays, solemnities, and special feasts, we bless God for the marvels of creation that bring so much goodness into the world and into our lives. The canticle begins: "Bless the Lord, all you works of the Lord. Praise and exalt him above all forever."[5] And with the naming of each element of creation, we then recite "bless the Lord." As another example, we

---

4. David Whyte, *Consolations: The Solace, Nourishment and Underlying Meaning of Everyday Words* (Langley, WA: Many Rivers Press, 2015), 89.

5. Sunday, Morning Prayer, Week 1. Because of the frequency and familiarity with which a deacon or priest prays with the current edition of the Psalms and Canticles in the Liturgy of the Hours, all of the texts from the Liturgy of the Hours in this book are taken from the International Commission on English in the Liturgy translation of *The Liturgy of the Hours*, 4 vols. (1974).

read in Psalm 28 (vv. 6-7): "Blessed be the Lord for he has heard my cry, my appeal. The Lord is my strength and my shield; in him my heart trusts. I was helped, my heart rejoices and I praise him with my song."[6] In Psalm 68 (v. 19), we pray: "May the Lord be blessed day after day. He bears our burdens, God our savior."[7] Every Monday during Evening Prayer, we recite the christological hymn of St. Paul that begins: "Praised be the God and Father of our Lord Jesus Christ, who has bestowed on us in Christ every spiritual blessing."[8] More recent translations of that text begin with the words "Blessed be the God and Father of our Lord Jesus Christ."[9]

The repeated praying of words such as these ought to infuse within the heart and mind of the pray-er a fundamental posture of *eucharistein* (giving thanks). In this way, the Liturgy of the Hours assists each deacon and priest in entering into the Liturgy of the Eucharist with a spirituality that truly opens up the essential eucharistic action of blessing God for what has been received. What is prayed in the Liturgy of the Hours so often allows the deacon and priest to enter more deeply and more authentically into the ritual words quoted at the beginning of this chapter that are prayed in the Liturgy of the Eucharist: "Blessed are you, Lord God of all creation, for through your goodness we have received the bread we offer you . . . the wine we offer you." While only the priest recites those words, the deacon and congregation join in the response "Blessed be God for ever." Furthermore, the presiding priest draws the deacon and congregation into the inherent thanksgiving dimension of blessing God with the Preface Dialogue. The presider says: "Let us give thanks to the Lord our God," to which all respond, "It is right and just."

---

6. Friday, Daytime Prayer, Week 1.
7. Tuesday, Office of Readings, Week 3.
8. Monday, Evening Prayer, all 4 Weeks.
9. See *New American Bible Revised Edition* and *New Revised Standard Version Bible*.

Our blessing of God gains us entrance into the very heart and mind of Christ as revealed throughout his public ministry and in the table fellowship he shared with his followers. Jesus received his life, his disciples, and his mission as a gift from the Father. After sending his disciples out on mission, then welcoming them back and offering them further teachings, Jesus prays with gratitude: "I give praise to you, Father, Lord of heaven and earth, for although you have hidden these things from the wise and the learned you have revealed them to the childlike. Yes, Father, such has been your gracious will. All things have been handed over to me by my Father" (Matt 11:25-27). Just before his death, Jesus acknowledges that his disciples have been the Father's gift to him.[10] Hence, in Christ, who is the paradigmatic deacon and priest, we see that gratitude is the manner in which our lives and ministries, which are themselves gifts from God, in turn become the means by which we bless God. Living in gratitude becomes the fundamental stance of our lives. Ronald Rolheiser goes so far as to maintain: "To give thanks, to be properly grateful, is the most primary of all religious attitudes. Proper gratitude is the ultimate virtue. It defines sanctity. Saints, holy persons, are people who are grateful, people who see and receive everything as gift."[11]

Gratitude to God for all that is received allows every aspect of our lives to be sublated from being something merely experienced to something truly received. Our thankfulness transforms the narrative elements (good or bad, painful or positive) within the plot that has unfolded in our lives—elements which we may not have reflected upon at the time—into recognized moments of grace which have helped to transform us into the members of the church we are today. Our prior action of attentively receiving our lives from God allows us to become aware that God has always been with us in everything we have endured and experienced as

10. See John 17:24.
11. Ronald Rolheiser, *Our One Great Act of Fidelity: Waiting for Christ in the Eucharist* (New York: Doubleday, 2011), 104.

all that we have needed God to be in the moment. This recognition of grace can stir in us as thankful hearts that feel "it is right and just" to bless the Lord our God in the eucharistic celebration and in our daily prayer. Furthermore, our attentiveness that leads to gratitude further allows the Holy Spirit to claim each and every aspect of our lives and sublate them from merely being something that happened *to us* into some way that God has been at work *in us*, slowly over time shaping us into the men God called to serve.

With this understanding of how attentiveness to grace in our "taking" becomes gratitude to God in our "blessing," we can recognize the deeper reality of every experience in life, no matter how joyful or positive, extraordinary or mundane it might be. In blessing God we know the truth within the following assertions:

- Harsh memories are sublated into the places where God's healing energy is at work in our hearts, minds, and spirits.

- Regrets and losses are transformed into moments of insight and true self-knowledge that come from God.

- Hurtful encounters and painful experiences are elevated into the entryways of wisdom and strength from the Holy Spirit.

- Joyful everyday moments of laughter and delight become the place of communion with the wondrous sacred moments when Christ "rejoiced [in] the Holy Spirit" (Luke 10:21).

- The thrill of being loved and of giving love becomes a sacrament of the very self-giving of God, who is love for us.

- Offering forgiveness and receiving forgiveness, even the struggle to forgive, are all signs of the Holy Spirit trying to unite us to the merciful heart of Christ.

- All the circumstances that forced us to let go of who we thought we were meant to be, what we thought we could accomplish, and what we hoped to achieve were all moments of intimacy with the dying of Christ that have led us to surrender into the hands of the Father who knows who we truly are and who created our true self that lies deep within us.

No matter what has unfolded in the story of our lives, all of it becomes the plot development within a narrative of grace and gratitude. When we are firmly grounded in this insight about our personal lives as men of God, then our pastoral lives as deacons and priests reveal the graced narratives of the communities with whom we celebrate the Eucharist. As deacons and priests, the Eucharist is to enkindle in us a capacity to bless God gratefully for the people we serve in our places of ministry. The eucharistic community with whom we celebrate is also a means of God's grace entering in our lives. As discussed in the previous chapter, the particularities of the parish, school, prison, hospital, nursing home, religious community, or other place of diaconal or priestly service are all contained within the bread and wine we "take" from them during the liturgy. Every person that constitutes the make-up of our worshipping community is brought forth in the bread and wine that we receive from them. And within that taking/receiving is our attentiveness to all the ways that the Holy Spirit, through our experiences with these people, draws out from us our consecrated unity with Christ the deacon and Christ the priest. This becomes a crucial dimension within our desire to bless God.

- We bless God for the sages in our community who have taught us how to access the wisdom of the Holy Spirit to handle difficulties and problems.

- We praise God for the living examples of fidelity and love, in good times and in bad, in sickness and in health, that have evoked in us a greater desire to be faithful in love to God, to our community, to our loved ones, including (for those who are married clergy) to our spouses.

- We give thanks that God has brought us companions for the mission in the wonderful staff members and volunteers who assist us in our duties.

- We bless God for those who make us laugh, those who make us think, those who are so life-giving when we are with them, and those who force us to go deeper into ourselves to find the patience or understanding that come from the Spirit of Christ.

- We praise God for the folks who have great new ideas, those who hold firm to the traditions of our faith community, and those who are the quiet mystics in our midst.

- We thank God for every encounter and experience within this eucharistic community because somehow each one of them was another means by which God, "who has begun the good work in us," was bringing it to fulfillment.

Admittedly, not every encounter with the people within our community feels like a blessing; not every moment is readily recognized as graced. With some people and in some circumstances, it can be very difficult to access a sense of gratitude to God. However, our repeated celebrations of the Eucharist seek to evoke such gratitude from us. In his article "All Is Grace," Henri Nouwen reminds us that true gratitude is not only gratefulness for the good things in life but an ability to say "everything is grace." While he focuses on one's personal narrative, Nouwen's words offer much insight about our stories as ordained clergy. He writes:

> Gratitude in its deepest sense means to live life as a gift to be received gratefully. But gratitude as the gospel speaks about it embraces *all* of life: the good and the bad, the joyful and the painful, the holy and the not so holy. . . . Is it truly possible to embrace with gratitude all of our life and not just the good things that we like to remember? . . . I am gradually learning that the call to gratitude asks us to say "everything is grace."

When our gratitude for our past is only partial, our hope for a new future can never be full. As long as we remain resentful about things that we wish had not happened, about relationships that we wish turned out differently, about mistakes we wish we had not made, part of our hearts remains isolated, unable to bear fruit in the new life ahead of us. If we are to be truly ready for a new task in the service of God, truly joyful at the prospect of a new vocation, truly free to be sent into a new mission, our entire past, gathered into the spaciousness of a converted heart, must become the energy that moves us toward the future.[12]

Nouwen echoes the strong contention of Ignatius of Loyola that an important goal of the spiritual life is to "find God in *all* things," not just *some* things or *most* things. That is true eucharistic gratitude which blesses God.

A final aspect of this act of giving thanks is that we also bless God not only for our community but also on behalf of our community for all the graces that have been in their lives, for which they are grateful. We bless God for all the joy, hope, love, laughter, friendship, and inner peace that our people have experienced personally and privately. We bless God for the moments they reconciled with estranged loved ones or friends, the times they found fortitude and strength to deal with difficulties and struggles, the insights they came to in their prayer and pondering, and the many ways they were for each other a tangible sign of God's loving companionship. Finally, we bless God for what God has been for our people in ways they cannot or do not express to others but which they recognize very really and tangibly, deep within their own hearts and inner spirits.

When members of the community place the bread and wine into our hands as deacons and priests, in essence they are entrusting to us all the ways that their human lives have been touched by

---

12. Henri Nouwen, "All Is Grace," *Weavings* 7 (November–December 1992): 38–41.

the goodness of God. Just as the bread and wine are the combination of the fruit of the earth/vine that come from our Creator and the work of human hands, so too are the lives of our people (and our own lives as well) the constant blending of human endeavor and divine grace. Rightfully, therefore, in blessing God during the preparation of the gifts within the Liturgy of the Eucharist, the priests prays, "through *your* goodness, we have received the bread[/wine] we offer you" (emphasis added). Our previous attentiveness to the God-dimension of every particularity of our lives, our people, our church that we have received, now becomes heart-filled gratitude for all that God has been for us, for our community, and for all of God's people.

Prayer and Reflection (Option A)

Take a few moments of silent reflection.
Prayerfully ponder the following:

1. Ask the Holy Spirit for a grateful heart.

2. Do a review of some of the more significant experiences of your life. Allow the Holy Spirit to lead you to an awareness of all the ways that God was for you what you needed God to be but might not have been aware of at the time of the experience.

3. Offer thanks to God for all that he has been for you in those experiences.

4. End by praying Psalm 34

Prayer and Reflection (Option B)

Take a few moments of silent reflection.
Prayerfully ponder the following:

1. Ask the Holy Spirit for a grateful heart.

2. Do a review of some of the more significant experiences in your place of ministry. Allow the Holy Spirit to lead you to an awareness of the graces of God that have come to you through the people you have encountered and the different moments of ministry you have exercised with them and for them.

3. Offer thanks to God for those graces.

4. End by praying the *Magnificat* of Mary

Blessing as Deepened Assent to Live in Covenant with God

Since, as ordained clergy, the Holy Spirit has been claiming our story and drawing it into the story of Jesus, then that defines the sense of gratitude by which we bless God as something more than mere human emotion. The Holy Spirit sublates our gratitude into communion with the heart of Christ whose own grateful blessing of God in his life and death constitute the terms of the new covenant. By our own acts of blessing God in communion with Christ, we are giving our assent to living the covenant with God in union with the self-giving and self-emptying of Christ. This becomes solid ground in our spiritual lives when we have come to recognize that God has always been with us as love in everything that we have experienced. We are able to join Christ in his complete surrender to the Father because we share in Christ's awareness of the magnitude and constancy of the Father's love for us in all things.

Once again, the Liturgy of the Hours assists us in our spiritual journey toward this felt awareness and experience of God's love. In particular, in saying Morning Prayer we often recite these words of the psalmist (Ps 63:2-5, 8):

> O God, you are my God, for you I long;
> for you my soul is thirsting.
> My body pines for you like a dry, weary land without water.
> So I gaze on you in the sanctuary
> to see your strength and your glory.
> For you love is better than life,
> my lips will speak your praise.
> So I will bless you all my life, in your name I will lift up my hands.
> My soul shall be filled as with a banquet,
> my mouth shall praise you with joy. . . .
> My soul clings to you;
> your right hand holds me fast.[13]

Jesus, who would have known all the psalms by heart, would have fervently "prayed into" this psalm at some point in his several hours on the cross. The recognition that the Father's love was better than life itself would have allowed Jesus to surrender in gratitude his entire self into the Father's hands. On the cross, Jesus blesses God and defines the new covenant.

In our blessing of God within the eucharistic liturgy we commit ourselves not only to an attentiveness to God's love in our lives but to an approach to life and ministry that is defined by this new covenant in Christ. We assent to live and minister essentially as men of self-surrender in gratitude and love to God. Furthermore, we assent to live and minister as men of self-giving to the needs of

13. Sunday, Morning Prayer, Week 1, as well as all solemnities and some major feasts.

God's people. This is what constitutes the "Offertory" of the liturgy. The priest prays over the gifts by indicating that they are "bread/wine we offer you"; the "you," of course, being God. The deacon's (and people's) response of "Blessed be God forever" constitute with the priest a willingness to offer all that they are to the Lord. This ritual exchange during the liturgy expresses our consent to allow the Holy Spirit to claim us so powerfully that our own hearts, minds, and wills are sublated into the heart, mind, and will of Christ the deacon and Christ the priest; in this way, everything we are is offered within the offering of Christ to God on behalf of the church. Our identity and our ministry as servant-leaders of the church become a blessing of God in Christ. However, this is the result of a long process that has been occurring well before the particular eucharistic liturgy we might be celebrating at any given moment. This process goes all the way back to our ordination.

The ritual of our ordination was only the beginning of this journey into becoming a blessing of God as a deacon or priest; it was not the sealed completion of that process. It would be good for us to remember this always, especially every time we engage in the ritual of preparing the bread and wine at the altar and praying over the gifts. That brief moment in the Liturgy of the Eucharist ought to make us cognizant of the need to be claimed more and more by the Holy Spirit who is about to claim the bread and wine in front of us in order to transform them into the presence of Christ. As we bless God for the fruits of the earth/vine and the work of human hands, we assent to covenant with Christ in his self-emptying within our own identity as a deacon or priest, an identity that is still being transformed by the fruits of the Holy Spirit and continually being shaped by the work we do in our lives as ordained servant-leaders in the church.

Self-emptying does not always come easy for men, no matter how well-trained we are in theology nor how long we have been ordained. It is so counter-intuitive to give up control over our lives when everything in our culture defines and rewards men for their ability to control the circumstances in which they find themselves in order to achieve a desired goal out of them. Our whole sense of self for the first half of our lives was constituted by the goals we sought to accomplish—goals that were defined mostly by the expectations of those who had (and might still have) moral, psychological, and emotional authority in our lives. When we have met those goals, we have been rewarded and our ego-identity more firmly established. This is an important part of our process of becoming who we are meant to be, but it is not the conclusion, for, in all of this, we are living our lives from the outside in, trying to be in sync with the expectations of others, which might be perfectly decent and honorable expectations. However, meeting those expectations is not necessarily a surrender to the voice of God within—the inner promptings of the Holy Spirit who knows the true self deep inside of us and who beckons us from within to surrender all that we have been (our false self) to the person God knows us truly to be. This true self is our deepest identity wonderfully and authentically yoked to Christ.[14]

To be yoked to Christ as our true self is to be joined in his complete self-emptying and surrender to God. Therefore, it is good for us to pray the words of St. Paul (Phil 2:5-11), who reminds deacons and priests every time we recite Sunday, Evening Prayer I:

> Have among yourselves the same attitude that is also yours in
> Christ Jesus,
> Who, though he was in the form of God,
> did not regard equality with God something to be grasped.
> Rather, he emptied himself,
> taking the form of a slave,
> coming in human likeness;
> and found human in appearance,
> he humbled himself,

14. For a thorough presentation on the false self and the true self see Richard Rohr's *Immortal Diamond: Our Search for Our True Self* (San Francisco: Jossey-Bass, 2013), 1–57.

becoming obedient to death,
even death on a cross.
Because of this, God greatly exalted him
and bestowed on him the name
that is above every name,
that at the name of Jesus
every knee should bend,
of those in heaven and on earth and under the earth,
and every tongue confess that
Jesus Christ is Lord,
to the glory of God the Father.

The *kenosis* (Greek word for self-emptying) of Christ described by Paul is a complete surrender to God. Jesus' surrender arises from his authentic sense of self that is completely known and loved by the Father and totally in sync with the Holy Spirit. Our own *kenosis* is not so complete; most certainly there are still things about ourselves, elements within our life's story, goals and ambitions we cling to which we have not yet surrendered to God. However, the ritual of the Eucharist keeps challenging us and assisting us to grow into the *kenosis* of Christ.

We will sense this challenge and grace when we pray well the brief but profound liturgical moment when the deacon (or priest, in the deacon's absence) prepares the chalice for the eucharistic prayer. He pours a drop of water into the wine as he prays: "By the mystery of this water and wine may we come to share in the divinity of Christ who humbled himself to share in our humanity." The self-emptying of Christ was his self-giving into the very real "stuff" of humanity in general, as well as into the very real particularities of each of our human lives. That comingling of water into wine signifies the eternal mystery of Christ who is constantly receiving into himself the very real "stuff" of our lives. This comingling in Christ beckons for us to allow all that comprises our lives—all that we are—to be comingled into Christ's complete self-offering to the Father for the sake of the church. As deacons and priests at the altar, we are not just preparing the contents of the chalice to be offered to God wholeheartedly; we are also preparing the content of our lives—the *entire* content of our lives—to be offered to God in union with the self-surrender of Christ. We can certainly acknowledge this surrender in faith, but to assent to it in our heart, mind, and will is a challenge.

Our own hesitancy in surrender recalls the exchange between Jesus and the earnest young man who genuinely seems to want to become a disciple. Mark's gospel is the first to recount the story of the rich youth who is truly devoted to living the commandments in order to attain the honorable goal of inheriting eternal life. He approaches Jesus. Then, "Jesus, looking at him, loved him and said to him, 'You are lacking in one thing. Go, sell what you have, and give to [the] poor and you will have treasure in heaven; then come, follow me.' At that statement his face fell, and he went away sad, for he had many possessions" (Mark 10:21-22). The young man—the paradigmatic good person who is still in the false self stage of life—seems sincerely to want to attain salvific union with God, but he wants to do so without a complete surrender to God. Only that surrender aligns him with Jesus Christ; only that all-encompassing *kenosis* is entrance into the kingdom of God. Without it, it would be "easier for a camel to pass through [the] eye of [a] needle" (Mark 10:25) than for one to strive to live the covenant of Christ without the surrender of all things to God. As mentioned earlier in this chapter regarding gratitude, so too with the notion of surrender, the challenge to give over to God *all* things does not mean *some* things or even *most* things.

Using as backdrop the story of the rich young man and how the would-be disciple walks sadly away from Jesus, Ronald Rolheiser writes about the importance of crossing the threshold from surrendering most of ourselves to surrendering all of ourselves to God.

> Concretely, that means giving over those last, clung-to areas of our lives . . . that last 10 percent we are still keeping to ourselves because we need those compensations to handle our tensions. And the sadness that so subtly clings to us like an

odor, even in our goodness and generosity, is there because, like the rich young man, we are still walking away from the full invitation. We are still holding something back, still holding on to some of our own riches.[15]

In the Liturgy of the Eucharist, we do not hold back a portion of the bread or wine from the blessing of God by taking only some of the eucharistic elements to the altar while leaving some of them off to the side or sending some of them back with the gift-bearers. Likewise, we do not accept only a percentage of the collection as an offering to God for the well-being of God's people but then send the rest back to congregation. Such actions within the liturgy would be alarming and blatantly improper, to say the least. In a similar vein, therefore, as deacons and priests who receive and then take these offerings—*all* of these offerings—to the altar, we ought to be challenged to participate in the offering more authentically by giving our entire selves to God. Our ritual participation in the acceptance and preparation of the gifts during the liturgy calls for us to develop in our spiritual lives a more complete participation in the *kenosis* of Christ. The celebration of the Eucharist that occurs so frequently in our lives needs to become the means by which the Holy Spirit claims all of our lives bit by bit, piece by piece, each part of our hearts, minds, and wills. In this way, the Spirit enables us to hold nothing of ourselves back from our surrender to God. Our priestly and diaconal roles in offering to God the gifts of the people needs to be a sacramental enactment of our own growing desire and capacity to offer all that we are, all that we have, and all that we do in union with Christ as a self-giving to God for the sake of the church.

In this way, the liturgical preparation of the gifts and the prayers over the gifts become the spiritually effective assent to give our lives completely as a deacon-in-Christ and a priest-in-Christ. This

---

15. Ronald Rolheiser, *Sacred Fire: A Vision for a Deeper Human and Christian Maturity* (New York: Image Books, 2014), 141–42.

constitutes our acceptance to live the new covenant in Christ which is always a *kenosis*, always a deeper intimacy with the heart and mind and will of Christ, which means, a never-ending process of sublation whereby the false self we once were becomes the true self we were made to be. It is that true self deep inside of us that the Holy Spirit claimed at our ordination and keeps drawing out from inside of us. It is that true self by which we bless God in our priestly and diaconal lives.

Additionally, we offer with ourselves the entirety of the people within our eucharistic community, keeping nothing and no one from God. Our model for this is, of course, Jesus himself. As he moves toward Jerusalem—the place of his complete self-offering— Jesus says, "I will draw everyone to myself" (John 12:32). Later, just before his death, Jesus prays to the Father in gratitude for the ones whom the Father has brought to him, saying: "I revealed your name to those whom you gave me out of the world. They belonged to you, and you gave them to me . . . . I pray for them . . . be- cause they are yours, and everything of mine is yours and every- thing of yours is mine, and I have been glorified in them. . . . and none of them was lost except the son of destruction, in order that the scripture might be fulfilled" (John 17:6, 9-10, 12). In the same manner, as deacons-in-Christ and priests-in-Christ, we are to pray to the Father our own offering of the entirety of our people as we move to the altar—the sacramental place of Christ's com- plete self-offering and our own. As noted in the previous chapter, everything and everyone that constitutes our community of min- istry has been brought forward in the bread and wine and received by us to be passed through our hearts before being placed on the altar. Immediately after this eucharistic action, in covenant with Christ, we draw all the people and everything about the people into ourselves and place all this in offering as we bless God through what we have taken/received.

In placing the gifts on the altar and praying over them, we are in actuality offering our own litany of blessing to the Lord that echoes the Prayer of the Three Young Men (Daniel 3:56-88) we recite so often in Morning Prayer.[16] As mentioned earlier in this chapter, that prayer affirms that every element of God's creation blesses the Lord, those things that we tend to experience in a positive way and those things that evoke negative reactions. From this perspective, the Prayer of the Three Young Men proclaims that, while the sun, the moon and stars, the majestic mountains, and the needed sources of water, warmth and food "praise and exalt God above all forever," so too do fire, ice, chill, snow, darkness, lightning and wild beasts bless the Lord. Therefore, our own eucharistic litany that we can pray deep inside of us as deacons and priests could be something like this:

> All of our people's "joys and hopes, the grief and anguish,"[17] whether they be known or remain hidden, bless the Lord.
>
> The needs of God's people just now expressed in the general intercessions, but also the yearnings so deep inside of them that they could never be spoken, bless the Lord.
>
> The persons who energize us and those who deplete us, bless the Lord.
>
> Those who make it so easy to be with them and those who make it so difficult, bless the Lord.
>
> The movers and shakers of this community, but also the disenchanted and the disengaged from the parish, bless the Lord.
>
> The older members who have been in the community a long time as well as the newest members who might not yet have fully cast their lot with this community, bless the Lord.
>
> Our community's past, unedited; its present, unfiltered; and its future, unknown, bless the Lord.

16. It is the Old Testament Canticle for Sunday, Morning Prayer, Week 1, and for all major solemnities.

17. The opening words of Vatican II's pivotal document *Gaudium et Spes* (Pastoral Constitution on the Church in the Modern World). Quotations of Vatican II documents are taken from Austin Flannery, ed., *Vatican Council II: Constitutions, Decrees, Declarations; The Basic Sixteen Documents* (Collegeville, MN: Liturgical Press, 2014).

All the celebrated milestones that have taken place within this community but also all the burdensome millstones that weigh heavily in their lives, bless the Lord.

The faith and commitment of these people gathered around us, but also the doubts, fears, and hesitations that lie within them, bless the Lord.

The pride in some about being Catholic but also the courage in others who are struggling with their anger at the church right now; bless the Lord.

Our people's contributions of time, treasure, and talents but also their own forms of reluctance to surrender to God, bless the Lord.

Those who are energetic, vibrant, physically strong as well as those who are diminished, depleted, or disabled in any way, bless the Lord.

In all that our people are, in all that they offer and in all that they hold within themselves, in all that they strive for and in all that they fail at, in all that they know and all that they still need to learn, in all the ways they demonstrate faith and all the deeper conversions that still need to occur, praise and exalt God above all forever.

This litany of offering that blesses God could add many more tropes. The point is that our assent to the new covenant in Christ means that with Christ we draw into our eucharistic offering everyone and everything within the community we serve and within the larger church as well. We do this as deacons and priests configured to Christ, about whom we pray every Wednesday evening in the Liturgy of the Hours: "It pleased God to make absolute fullness reside in him and, by means of him, to reconcile everything in his person, both on earth and in the heavens, making peace through the blood of his cross" (Col 1:19-20). In Christ's own complete self-offering on the cross is everyone and everything that has come from God. The totality of his *kenosis* includes the totality of creation. As ordained deacons and priests, our own *kenosis* in Christ is to include not only our total self but also the entirety of the people and church we serve. In this way, through our diaconal and priestly roles in the eucharistic offering, the full reality of our people is drawn so intimately into Christ. Thus, we see that our taking/ receiving all the particularities of our community then becomes our offering of all the graced aspects of these particularities as our blessing of God. But this never means that we whitewash these particularities as if, somehow, we can only bless God by removing what has been difficult, painful, or disappointing in what we have experienced. Quite the opposite is true: what is graced by God is also always broken as well.

While grace is to be found in each and every one of the particularities of human life, so too does brokenness affect each and every human experience. God's grace and human brokenness always coincide. Thus, our gratitude to God and our blessing of God within the Eucharist are never denials of the real brokenness in people's lives, in the church and the world, nor in ourselves. Instead, the Eucharist celebrates our firm belief that within Christ's very personhood (his real presence), which is the very center of the Eucharist, the realities of God's grace and human brokenness are always joined together. Christ's very personhood is the nexus of blessing and breaking; and as deacons and priests configured more deeply to Christ, we are to carry deep inside of us that nexus point on behalf of our people.

Ritually this happens as the liturgy progresses from the preparation of the gifts into the eucharistic prayer. The priest invites the people through the Preface Dialogue to "lift up [their] hearts" and then to "give thanks to the Lord our God." The deacon, leading the response of the people, then says, "It is right and just." Then all join together in praising God and singing a *hosanna* blessing of "he who comes in the name of the Lord." It is truly right and just that our blessing of God becomes aligned to Christ whose narrative forever joins God's grace and human brokenness. Christ does this most fully on the cross, when the body of Christ is broken and his love is poured out for us. Thus, the Liturgy of the Eucharist moves from blessing to breaking, especially within the institution narrative of the eucharistic prayer. Gerhard Lohfink, in his wonderful treatise on a theology of prayer, writes this about the eucharistic prayer: "The 'account of institution' is thanksgiving above all because it interprets the death of Jesus as a saving event: 'given up for you,' 'poured out for the many,' as the prayer says. . . . The so-called 'words of institution' are located within a story, a report, and that report functions not simply as reportage but as thanksgiving to God for Jesus' sacrifice of his life."[18] Not only does God bless *us* (i.e., God saves us) through the death of Christ, but in the broken body and poured out blood of Christ is our own blessing of God (i.e., we give thanks and praise to God).

Within the Liturgy of the Eucharist, as the narrative moves from taking and blessing into breaking and giving, we recognize that our gratitude to God includes our recognition that what God does for us in Christ happens in the midst of what is broken and bruised in life, not in spite of it. So too our capacity to give ourselves with Christ to God and to God's people includes the brokenness we hold within us. That is why the eucharistic narrative that claims us does not end with the verb "bless." As the story of Jesus unfolds within the Eucharist and within us, the narrative of our lives moves on from "take" and "bless" and continues on with "break" and "give." We will now examine how what we "take" and "bless" becomes sublated into the broken body of Christ in order to be given as the blessing of Christ's presence for the world. As we will explore in the chapters ahead, the more *receptive* eucharistic actions of "taking" and "blessing" become the more *generative* eucharistic actions of "breaking" and "giving." This guarantees that the eucharistic story claiming us as deacons and priests does not remain a hidden narrative inside of us. It is a narrative that is witnessed as it enfolds within it the lives of all of God's people whom we serve as ordained men of the church.

---

18. Gerhard Lohfink, *Prayer Takes Us Home: The Theology and Practice of Christian Prayer* (Collegeville, MN: Liturgical Press, 2020), 183.

Prayer and Reflection (Option A)

Take a few moments of silent reflection.
Prayerfully ponder the following:

1. Ask the Holy Spirit for the graces of honesty and surrender.

2. Read the Story of the Rich Young Man in Mark 10:17-31. Imagine yourself in the scene. Recall that Mark says Jesus looked at the man with love.
   - Knowing Christ loves you, be open to what he might be asking you to surrender in order to follow him more completely.
   - About which struggles with surrendering completely to God is Jesus challenging you?
   - Is he revealing to you an issue you might have with vulnerability or control?

3. Take an honest look at your own life patterns to recognize how, where, and when are you still holding back parts of yourself and your life from your surrender to God.

4. Ask Jesus to help you embrace his own surrender to God.

5. End by praying the "Suscipe" of St. Ignatius of Loyola:

   > Take, Lord, and receive all my liberty,
   > my memory, my understanding,
   > and my entire will,
   > all I have and call my own.
   >
   > You have given all to me.
   > To you, Lord, I return it.

> Everything is yours; do with it what you will.
> Give me only your love and your grace,
> that is enough for me.

Prayer and Reflection (Option B)

Take a few moments of silent reflection.
Prayerfully ponder the following:

1. Ask the Holy Spirit for the graces of honesty and surrender.

2. Pray with the words of Jesus in his final prayer to the Father in John 17 in which he offers to the Father all those who were given to him.
   - What part of Jesus' prayer do you resonate with? Why?
   - What part of Jesus' prayer do you struggle with? Why?
   - Invite Jesus to talk with you about what was in his own heart and mind in praying those words just before his complete self-offering on the cross.
   - Invite Jesus to help you with any form of self-offering you struggle with in your place of ministry or with certain persons or groups in ministry.

3. Consider the following:
   - Are there people in your place of ministry who are difficult for you to draw to yourself or to draw into your prayer?

- Are there people in your place of ministry or on the peripheries of your place of ministry whom you never thought of drawing into your prayer before but you are now aware of?
- Who are the persons who are coming to you right now in your heart and mind that you want to bring to God in prayer?

4. Ask Jesus to help you embrace in your ministry his own gratitude for all those whom God brought to him in his public ministry.

5. Pray the words of Jesus in John 17:6-26.

chapter five

BREAK

For as often as you eat this bread and drink the cup, you proclaim the death of the Lord until he comes.

—1 Corinthians 11:26

The Eucharist Is Inherently Communion with Christ in His Brokenness

The varied meanings of the verb "to break" have been a part of our personal narratives throughout our lives. As children we were often warned not to break something in the house and, subsequently, we were scolded when we did. As we were growing up and learning to connect with others in friendship and affection, we discovered how painful it could be when our hearts were broken. As we have journeyed through adulthood, we have experienced broken promises and pledges, endured broken hopes and dreams, suffered broken relationships, and encountered broken people with broken spirits. As we have moved further into our own spiritual lives we have discovered that, no matter how successful or well put-together we appear on the outside, deep inside of us we can feel at times like a very broken person. Furthermore, as we have all been left reeling from the further revelations of sexual abuse by religious persons, we have been forced to admit with horror and despair that we are ordained ministers within a very broken church. It is clear, therefore, that "breaking" is not merely something we can do to precious things, fragile persons, and delicate relationships; "breaking" is also what original sin, human sin, and just plain life itself have done to our fragile lives, the delicate bonds we have forged with others, and the never-before-admitted fragility of our precious church. If these aspects of brokenness are not received attentively nor offered to God rightly, then all of these experiences of the varied connotations of what "broken" means can distance us from wanting to admit to our own brokenness and being able to experience the powerful reality of the brokenness of Jesus Christ in the Eucharist.

This attentive receiving of the fractured reality of our lives, our church, our people, our world leads to the blessing of God with these very same lives, church, people, and world. Furthermore, this attentive receiving and then grateful blessing of God is what draws us into communion with the moment when Christ's own life (received from the Father and given as a blessing in return to the Father) is broken on the cross. Once we have received our lives, our church, our people, our world as they truly are (which necessarily means the fractured narratives of every person and institution), then we can bless God for all that God has been in the midst of these broken realities because we have found God with us in them. At this point, we can profoundly discover that brokenness is precisely the place of intimate communion with Christ, whose own body is broken and life's blood poured out for us. This is how all the dyings-to-self we have endured in the fractured realities of life are joined to the death of Christ. It is the means by which the Holy Spirit sublates our human brokenness into, in the words of St. Paul quoted above, a proclamation of "the death of the Lord" every time we celebrate the Eucharist "until [Christ] comes again."

Our exercise of ministry, fed by the Eucharist, is to make what we do a proclamation of the death of the Lord and, at the same time, a revelation of Christ alive in all the brokenness to which we minister and out of which we minister. Our communion with the broken Christ is how the Eucharist helps to claim so much of what we are and what we do as deacons and priests. (1) The Eucharist shows us that we do not merely minister to the brokenness in people's lives; we minister to others *out of* our own brokenness. (2) We do not merely seek to alleviate the brokenness in the world (and the church); we seek to embrace the brokenness of the world (and the church) in order to draw it into the transforming grace of communion with Christ. (3) Lastly, we do not merely celebrate the Eucharist in order to receive for ourselves and distribute to others the broken body of Christ; we celebrate the Eucharist precisely as broken men who have been claimed by Christ whose own brokenness on the cross is redemptive for all.

While we might be able to offer an intellectual assent to such a theology of the Eucharist and ordination, which mean acknowledging with a certain level of rational comfort that our brokenness has to be part of the whole mix, allowing this assent to claim our personal narrative on an experiential level is a whole other matter. On that level, letting our fractured selves to be claimed by the eucharistic story of Jesus can be difficult; in fact, it can be *very* difficult, especially if we do not want to acknowledge our brokenness. This acknowledgement often comes only when we experience our own "Damascus" moment. Recall how St. Paul, on his way to Damascus, full of heroic archetypal energy in which he was going to save Judaism from the corrupt followers of the Nazarene, was knocked to the ground by a revelation from Christ. Headstrong in his determination to erase the disciples of Jesus from the children of Abraham, the once-named Saul hears the voice of Jesus as he reveals himself as the one whom Saul is persecuting. The risen Lord comes to Saul not in the appearance of a majestic God but as the plaintive voice of all those who have been persecuted by Saul's zeal and murderous threats.[1] This voice of brokenness literally and spiritually knocks Saul to the ground.

Later, St. Paul interprets this foundational moment of his life of ministry as something that God desired for him, writing: "[God],

---

1. See Acts 9:1-9.

who from my mother's womb had set me apart and called me through his grace, was pleased to reveal his Son to me, so that I might proclaim him to the Gentiles" (Gal 1:15). Paul had come to realize that he was a terribly broken man who had all along been loved by God, and in that love God was claiming his brokenness for the mission of the gospel. Look at how Paul describes himself as an apostle: "For I am the least of the apostles, not fit to be called an apostle, because I persecuted the church of God. But by the grace of God, I am what I am" (1 Cor 15:9-10). Paul acknowledges not only that he is a broken human being but that his brokenness has been claimed by the grace of God to make him who he now is. Most assuredly this was a sometimes painful and often difficult process in Paul's life.

It is a process that needs to happen in each of our lives. This has certainly been the case in my own personal life and in my years as a priest. As a young seminarian and then a newly ordained priest, I was full of youthful energy and untested zeal. So much of what I did and what I wanted to do was coming out of the archetypal heroic energy that wanted to achieve great things for Christ and for the church.[2] Within this archetypal energy were the ego-needs for success and recognition, the ego-strength of absolute certitude and headstrong determination, along with an underlying ego-assuredness that, with the right skills, the right work ethic, and the right focus, anything I sought to accomplish in ministry would happen. I was on a fully mounted ride to Damascus.

One year, when wholly caught up in the energy of this hero-for-Christ archetype, I made my annual silent, directed retreat. Because it was wintertime when I made my retreat, I was not housed in the regular retreat house that I had stayed at in previous years, since there were only a few retreatants that week. Instead, I was housed in

---

2. See my explanation of the major archetypal energies exhibited by seminarians and priests in my book *From Hero to Servant to Mystic: Navigating the Deeper Waters of Priestly Spirituality* (Collegeville, MN: Liturgical Press, 2019). These archetypes can easily be applied to the spiritual lives of deacons as well.

the building where the Jesuit community lived and where they also established an infirmary for their aging brothers. On the first day of my retreat, I headed to my director's office. I had to walk down a long corridor before making a turn down another corridor to his office. That first day of the retreat, as I walked down the hallway to meet my director, sitting right at the crossroads of the two corridors was an elderly Jesuit brother stooped over in a wheelchair. As I came closer, the sound of my footsteps must have alerted him to my approach for he straightened himself up in the chair and gave me a huge smile and a warm hello; then he fell back into his stooped posture. I said a quick hello and went to meet my director.

During our initial session, after my director's patient listening to all of my frustrations that things in ministry were not going the way I had wanted, the director told me that during my prayer times I need to ask Jesus to reveal himself to me. "Simple enough," I thought to myself, and immediately set off to accomplish—with certain success—the task I had been given. And that day nothing happened during my prayer periods. I kept trying to picture Jesus in my mind, recalling all the holy cards and works of art that portrayed the youthful, vital, serene and undaunted Jesus of Nazareth going about the mission for which he had been sent. But none of those images held in my prayer.

The next day I once again headed down the long hallway to go meet my director and once again the aging Jesuit brother was sitting stooped over in his wheelchair at the crossroads of the hallways. Just like the day before, as I came near, the elderly brother straightened himself up in his chair, mustered a warm smile and a gracious hello, and stooped back over in his chair as I passed by to get to my appointment. When I told my director that nothing had happened in my prayer periods, he told me to continue with the same task: "Ask Jesus to reveal himself to you." Off I went for *that* day's prayer periods, and again nothing happened. The next day, the same pattern. In the morning I headed off to my appointment with my director, passed by the elderly Jesuit stooped over in his wheelchair, exchanged greetings with him, and went in and told my director that nothing happened. He told me to just keep with the same task: "Ask Jesus to reveal himself to you." Again, nothing happened. As a matter of fact, nothing happened for six days.

It was now the last day of my retreat and I was very frustrated. In the morning, full of disappointment that the retreat was a waste of time, I headed down the hallway for my daily appointment. There, as every morning, was the elderly Jesuit stooped over in his wheelchair. As every morning, he straightened himself up to give me a greeting. Only, on that morning, after I greeted him and walked past him, as I turned down the adjacent corridor I heard as clear as a bell a voice inside of me say, "Scott, that was me!" I was spiritually knocked to the ground. To this day, I can still hear that voice inside of me saying, "Scott, that was me!"

As I have unpacked the meaning of that moment throughout the years, I have come to recognize that in my youthful exuberance I had been spending most of my retreat projecting onto Christ what I wanted to see in myself—youthful vitality, energetic zeal, a determined spirit, an able-bodied worker for the Lord. I was looking for a Christ who was a young man, full of energy, strength, and vibrancy. I was not yet at a place in my spiritual life where I could recognize and accept that I needed to connect with Christ in my brokenness, that is, my weaknesses and limitations, my helplessness and vulnerability. I certainly did not want to acknowledge that there could be something diminished, something weak, something stooped over in my capacity to be a hero-for-Christ. As that retreat experience revealed, until I could see my own brokenness, I could not yet see Christ. And so *Christ had to break open my brokenness by revealing his own*; he had to knock me to the ground and dislodge my headstrong fervor and determination by sending to me a stooped-over, aging, wheelchair-bound man of faith who clearly had the heart of God.

While that moment of more than thirty years ago still lives powerfully in me, it still took several years before I could embrace its meaning for myself and for priesthood. For a long time, I still operated out of the ego energy of self-determination, bumping up against the disappointments and failures of ministry so many times that I began to wonder if I should have been ordained a priest at all. However, slowly over time, the revelation of Christ in that hallway started to claim me more and more, drawing into the heart of God not only my sense of who I was as a beloved but broken child of God, but also how I was to minister as a priest. I have come to believe that "Scott, that was me" were the heartfelt words of Jesus who desired for me what he desired from Paul, a new foundation for the ministry to which I had been called. It was the presence of the One whom I encountered daily in the Eucharist. It was the gentle beckoning of the One calling me to continue to be a priest, but a priest who no longer operated from a place that sought accomplishment and success, rather an ordained minister motivated from a place of being sought out in love by Christ who came to me in brokenness in order to draw my own brokenness into communion with him. From that place of communion, Christ was calling me to minister to the brokenness in the world and people around me. As with St. Paul, my Damascus moment did not reveal a vision of a glorious God beyond my comprehension but rather the voice of a broken Jesus who knew my brokenness even before I did. And he loved me anyways. Like St. Paul who met the persecuted Christ, I met a messy Messiah.

The Sacred Supper of the Lord Is the Messy Meal of a Messy Messiah

Besides the admonitions in our childhood narrative not to break anything and the subsequent reprimands when we did, there were also the oft-repeated parental warnings not to spill anything when we were seated at the table and the ensuing admonishments when that, in fact, is precisely what we caused to happen. It is wonderfully ironic, therefore, (and a little bit amusing) to realize that, at the very core of the most important meal we share as Christian disciples, breakage and spillage are required. The Supper of the Lord is indeed a very messy meal, even as we regard it as supremely sacred.

As a sacred meal, the Eucharist comes from breakage; it is the body of Christ broken for us and given to us to eat, that is, to consume. Furthermore, the Eucharist emerges from spillage; it is the blood of Christ poured out—spilled—from his broken body and given to us to drink, that is, to be ingested into our very selves. Far from being the rigorous adherence to the rules of etiquette for a pristine dining experience, the Eucharist invites those who celebrate this supper to eat what is broken and drink what is spilled. Hence eating and drinking the body and blood of Christ become communion with the real brokenness of Christ. Christ's real presence in the Eucharist includes his intimate union with the messiness of human existence. Using the theology of St. Paul's Letter to the Corinthians quoted at the outset of this chapter, the Eucharist is our proclamation of faith that in the dying of Christ—in his brokenness—is to be found the true sustenance for our living. In this way, we proclaim the death of the Lord when our life is a personal joining of our brokenness with the brokenness of Christ. Our fractured narrative is drawn into Christ's sacred narrative of complete self-giving for our salvation. In Christ's personal story, his body is broken for us and his blood is spilled for us. But Christ's intimate union with the messiness of human life did not only take place within the messiness of Christ's passion that we remember in the Eucharist: the cross of Christ comes as the capstone of a whole lifetime of entering into redemptive union with the messiness of human life beginning with Jesus' conception and birth.

The incarnation of Jesus did not unfold as a story of an untarnished hero who lived a life of earthly grandeur but as the self-emptying of a God who loved us so much that God took on all the contours and all the dimensions of our broken human condition in order to save us. We all know the narrative so well because as deacons and priests we proclaim it constantly as the gospel during liturgy. During Advent, we proclaim how the incarnation begins as a pregnancy that raises suspicions of adultery against Mary and then needs to be handled justly and prudently by Joseph.[3]

3. See Matt 1:18-25.

Throughout the Christmas season, we proclaim how the incarnation continues as the birth of a child whose parents are displaced from their home, strangers in a strange land, and dependent on the assistance of others, which then sets up for the birth to occur in the filth and squalor of a stable full of animals.[4] The incarnation immediately draws toward it the lowly and poor shepherds who live on the margins of life[5] as well as non-believing dabblers in the occult (magi) who do not fit the mold of what adorers of God should be like.[6] As his death will be later, the birth of this messy Messiah evokes human treachery and violent killing—the worst of the proclivities in human brokenness.[7]

As the liturgical year progresses, we continue to proclaim the good news of how the incarnation of God draws to himself all forms of human messiness. From the outset, the Incarnate Son of God faces the temptations that all human beings face.[8] The gospel of the incarnate One includes numerous accounts of Jesus healing the sick, freeing the demonically possessed, and seeking out the unwanted and the unwelcomed. Furthermore, the gospel narrative describes repeatedly how Jesus offers forgiveness to sinners and even raises the dead to life again. And the gospel we deacons and priests proclaim captures in so many ways the teachings of Jesus who regards brokenness as beatitude;[9] who muddies the clarity of the Torah by stretching the limits of how people understood moral righteousness and Sabbath observance;[10] and who constantly calls his followers to identify with the last, the least, and the lost because

4. See Luke 2:1-7.

5. See Luke 2:8-18.

6. See Matt 2:1-12.

7. See the figure of Herod in Matt 2; and the prediction of Simeon in Luke 2:33-35.

8. See Matt 4:1-11; Mark 1:12-13; Luke 4:1-13.

9. See Matt 5:1-11 and Luke 6:20-22.

10. See especially the Sermon on the Mount (Matt 5-7), the Sermon on the Plain (Luke 6:17-49), and Jesus' confrontations with the scribes and Pharisees (among them, Matt 11:37-54; Matt 23; Luke 6:1-11).

in them is Jesus found.[11] In fact, the incarnation of Christ is so identified with human brokenness that, at one point, Jesus openly declares that he has come to make things messy:

> Do not think that I have come to bring peace upon the earth. I have come to bring not peace but the sword. For I have come to set
>   a man "against his father,
>   a daughter against her mother,
>   and a daughter-in-law against her mother-in-law;
>   and one's enemies will be those of his household." (Matt 10:34-36)

In the gospel narrative are experiences of Jesus being rejected in his own hometown, the painful loss of someone dear to him, malicious distortions about what he is doing, treachery and plotting against him, betrayal, abandonment by his closest friends, and deep agony over what his own impending death would entail.[12] The gospel writers also give us a glimpse into the interior life of Jesus as he draws the messiness of human life into his heart. For instance, we are told that when he sees the crowd of people before him who need to be healed and who need to be fed, he confesses to his disciples that his heart is moved with pity for them.[13] When the rich young man cannot give away his possessions to follow Jesus, he looks upon this would-be disciple with love.[14] And when Jesus encounters the deep grief of the sisters of Lazarus who has died, Jesus weeps and become perturbed in spirit.[15]

All of these details of Jesus' intimate communion with the messiness of human life are important plot points within the gospel of Christ that we priests and deacons *proclaim* during the Liturgy of the Word within the Eucharist. In turn, this sacred narrative now needs to *claim* the proclaimers; it needs to draw our own messy

---

11. Jesus identifies himself with the least ones in Matt 25:31-46.

12. See Mark 6:1-6; Matt 14:3-13; Mark 3:20-22; Mark 14:1-2; Mark 14:43-49; Mark 14:50; and Luke 22:39-46, respectively.

13. See Matt 15:32.

14. See Mark 10:21.

15. See John 11:1-44.

lives, our own messy parishes, our messy church and our messy world into intimacy with Christ's brokenness. This perspective allows us to understand that, while the Eucharist ought always to be celebrated with reverence, carefulness, and the "noble simplicity" called for by *Sacrosanctum Concilium* (34), the Eucharist is also a messy meal that renders as truly, really, substantially present Christ's entire life of embracing what needed to be healed, forgiven, and transformed in the messy, broken lives of God's beloved ones. Another way of stating this is that "the mess is in the meal" because it is a meal with Christ, our messy Messiah. Additionally, we can say that "the meal comes from the mess" because it comes from Christ, whose entire incarnation is an embrace of the broken human condition, including a painful, messy crucifixion which stands at the center of the meal.

In the Eucharist We Consume the Death of Christ

Lest we think that Christ's brokenness is merely tangential to our understanding of his real presence in the Eucharist, note that the institution narrative in most of the eucharistic prayers is introduced with a stark statement of the brokenness that Jesus experienced. The presider prays: "On the day before he was to suffer . . ." (Eucharistic Prayer I and all four versions of the Eucharistic Prayer of Various Needs); "At the time he was betrayed . . ." (Eucharistic Prayer II); "For on the night he was betrayed . . ." (Eucharistic Prayer III); "But before his arms were outstretched between heaven and earth . . ." (Eucharistic Prayer for Reconciliation I); "For when about to give his life to set us free . . ." (Eucharistic Prayer for Reconciliation II). The messy meal of the Eucharist is clearly about Jesus being broken by suffering and death. Therefore, ritually the meal that proclaims Christ's death does not consist of eating food that remains intact. Bread is broken to become our food. Likewise, the Eucharist is not a supper of temperance in which no alcohol is drunk. Wine is poured to become our drink. This meal sacramentalizes the death of Christ, for the only way Christ can be given to us as bread and wine is if he is broken and poured out in death. Thus, we "break" bread so that in eating it, we consume into our broken selves the broken Christ, the complete self-sacrifice of Christ in humility and in trust of the Father's love. We drink the "spilled" blood of Christ, his life force of love being emptied out of him, which is then slaked into the very empty, broken places in ourselves where we thirst for healing, forgiveness, transformation, and fulfillment.

However, even though the Eucharist is primarily a meal of Christ's death, it is at the same time a life-giving celebration. Only those who want to continue to live reach for food and drink to sustain themselves. And there cannot be life without the intake of food and drink. But ironically the life-giving power of food comes from some form of death, since all food at one time was in some manner a living thing, whether it be a plant, a grain, a fruit or vegetable, or an animal. In the Eucharist, the food is the person of Jesus Christ who completely surrenders to death on the cross. Just as all food is death in some way, so also all death is brokenness of some kind, whether it be due to illness, aging, an accident, suicide, or the treacherous actions of others. Thus, the death of Christ is both food and brokenness. More specifically, Christ's death is brokenness that has become food. Even more profoundly, because it is the death of the Incarnate Son of God, in Christ's death is God's salvific communion with all human experiences of death and dying, all moments of human brokenness and anguish. And this communion is life-giving.

To be sure, there is real and lasting life in Christ's death, but access to that life only comes from our own brokenness being brought into communion with Christ's brokenness. In the eucharistic narrative of our lives, this means that, after we have allowed ourselves to attentively take what constitutes our real lives and then bless God with a grateful awareness of all that God has been in the real "stuff" of our lives, we then can confidently recognize what is broken in us and unite it in trust and faith to the broken body and poured out blood of Christ. This involves so much more than just receiving the consecrated bread and wine at Communion time. It means consciously naming our brokenness and then allowing it to be claimed by the Spirit who draws it into communion with Christ on the cross. The eucharistic narrative in Mark's gospel allows us to unpack this dimension in the eucharistic narrative of our lives.

In his wonderful text, *The Eucharist in the New Testament and the Early Church*, Eugene LaVerdiere shows the great lengths to which Mark went to unite through the Eucharist the passion of Christ with the existential suffering of the Markan community.[16] The *haecceitas* of Mark's community was one of great anguish and desperation as they faced severe persecution from the Romans as retribution for the Jewish rebellion in the late 60s AD. As LaVerdiere writes: "Mark told the story of the Eucharist because it was an important part of the gospel; but even more importantly, he told the story because the community was in a period of crisis. The Eucharist would help them see the implications of the gospel at an important juncture in their history."[17] Therefore, Mark connects the Lord's Supper very intensely with the suffering and death of Christ. Very poignantly he teaches his community that their current passion is assumed (sublated) into the passion of Christ that is already unfolding within the Last Supper and is present every time the Lord's Supper is celebrated. "Mark's readers needed to see the full implications of the Eucharist as a sharing in the passion-resurrection of Christ."[18]

These implications are apparent in the context of the Lord's Supper that Mark offers. While all of the Synoptic gospel writers place the Lord's Supper within the context of the Passover, Mark gives greater focus on the context not merely being Jewish Passover but more specifically *Jesus'* Passover. As the feast of Unleavened Bread draws near, Jesus' disciples say to him: "Where do you want us to

---

16. Eugene Laverdiere, SSS, *The Eucharist in the New Testament and the Early Church* (Collegeville, MN: Liturgical Press, 1996), chap. 4, "In the Following of Christ: The Eucharist in Mark's Gospel," 46–64.

17. Laverdiere, 48.

18. Laverdiere, 59.

go and prepare for you to eat the Passover" (Mark 14:12)? They do not ask about a place for "us" to eat the Passover. Furthermore, Jesus instructs the disciples to tell the master of the house: "The Teacher says, 'Where is *my* guest room where *I* may eat the Passover with my disciples?'" (Mark 14:14).[19] For the Jews, Passover is a feast of liberation, "the feast of a God who makes it possible for life that has been crushed to rebound when set free."[20] But the ultimate liberation occurs in and through Christ. This is conveyed by the fact that no details of a true Passover meal are given, including the Passover lamb. The reason for this is that, for Mark, the Passover of Israel is fulfilled in Jesus (the Passover lamb), whose death and resurrection bring true liberation. The Passover is now happening in and through Jesus.

Mark further shows that, in this Passover, Christ assumes into himself all human anguish, suffering, and pain, that is, human brokenness. First of all, Mark does this by demonstrating that Jesus is enduring an inner passion that is followed by his outer passion and the Lord's Supper occurs right in the middle of them.[21] Mark divides his passion narrative into the "private passion" of Jesus (14:1-42) that happens inside of him and the "public passion" (14:43–15:47) that is beheld by the crowds in Jerusalem. The "private passion" reveals that Jesus goes to his death knowingly and deliberately. But this occurs after a deep interior struggle in which Jesus first rejects death and then comes to accept it resolutely as the will of his Father as Jesus emerges from his agony in the garden. Because of his internal struggle and then acceptance, Jesus is able freely to face his death—and do it alone—since all of his disciples abandoned him and fled (Mark 14:56).

Taking together all of the details of Mark's account of the Lord's Supper within his passion narrative, we can recognize that the

---

19. Emphasis added.
20. Xavier Léon-Dufour, SJ, *Sharing the Eucharistic Bread: The Witness of the New Testament* (New York: Paulist Press, 1987), 192.
21. See Léon-Dufour, 186–89.

eucharistic words of Jesus are not offered as a prescription for a future ritual that the disciples are to maintain. This is not Mark's concern since, by the time Mark wrote his gospel, the Eucharist was already a well-established ritual habit within Christian communities. Notice that, in Mark's account, there is no admonition by Jesus for the disciples to "Do this in remembrance of me." In addition, Mark does not construct the narrative pieces of the Lord's Supper merely to refer to a death of Jesus that is *going to* happen *after* the meal. The Greek present participle that Mark uses, *ekchynnomenon,* should rightly be translated "is *being* shed" here and now.[22] In Xavier Léon-Dufour's analysis of these words of institution, he concludes: "In the actions and words of the Supper Jesus is 'expressing' his death, he is 'experiencing.' A climax is reached here that cannot be surpassed: not only is Jesus aware of his coming death and consenting to it; his words freely make it already a fact."[23] In the meal is the very passion of Christ, his complete surrender in love to the Father, his total loving embrace of all human brokenness and death. In the Eucharist Jesus' death, by which he achieves communion with all human suffering, is here and now, to be consumed into the deepest interiority of all who partake of the Lord's Supper.

This understanding of the already well-established ritual of the Eucharist is important for Mark because he needs to deal with the present existential suffering of his community, that is, the very real passion and death of the Christians for whom he writes his gospel. The Markan community is experiencing both a private passion of internal anguish over what is happening to them, but also a public passion of persecution and displacement. They are to find a powerful oneness with the death of Christ, which is a present reality in their eucharistic feasts.

22. See endnote 8 in Léon-Dufour, 361.
23. Léon-Dufour, 188.

In the Eucharist Christ Unites with Our Own Brokenness so That We Are Transformed

In the "words of institution," Jesus establishes a reciprocal relationship between himself and the community of disciples (and, therein, Mark's community and all Christian communities who celebrate the Eucharist). His broken body and shed blood are given *to them*; therefore, they are to receive them. Note how Mark adds, "they all drank from [the cup]" (Mark 14:23). In receiving what Jesus gives in the Lord's Supper, all who partake of the bread and wine enter into Christ's salvific communion of being broken. The action of giving bread represents the action of Jesus giving himself in death. "Body" [the Greek *soma*] means one's personhood.[24] Thus, in giving his body, Jesus gives himself as being broken in suffering and death for all of us. In giving his blood, Jesus is giving his very life force poured out in love because it is blood that is "shed for many."[25]

The reciprocal relationship that Jesus establishes with his eucharistic self-giving is meant to claim his disciples and eventually transform them and the world through them. As is clear from the rest of Mark's account of the Lord's Supper, the meal with Jesus transforms not only broken bread and poured out wine but also broken disciples who struggle to pour themselves out in complete devotion to Christ. The Eucharist does not eliminate human brokenness; it engages it in order to transform it. Look further at Mark's account: The disciples, who are about to stumble in the

---

24. See Léon-Dufour, 119: "When Semites use the word 'body,' they are not referring to the organism that is at the human being's disposal, but rather to the person insofar as it is able to express and manifest itself, or to the person insofar as it enters into relations with the universe and with other human beings. In biblical anthropology, human beings do not merely have bodies, they *are* bodies. Therefore, since Jesus, like every other human being, expresses himself through his body, the expression 'my body' refers to his person insofar as it is related in a concrete way to other human beings and to the whole of creation."

25. See Léon-Dufour, 143: "In general, blood is regarded in the Bible as 'the soul of the life' and belongs to God alone."

unfolding of Jesus' passion, still declare themselves ready to receive all that Christ is by their partaking in the bread and wine. For instance, Peter and the rest of the disciples declare their readiness to die with Jesus (Mark 14:31). By the time of the writing of Mark's gospel, this is historical fact. Yet, as the story unfolds, all the disciples abandon Jesus when he is arrested, and Peter goes so far as to deny even knowing Jesus.[26] Thus, the exchange between Jesus and the disciples during their last meal together could be Mark's way of assuring the members of his community of the transformative power of the Eucharist during the difficulties that they face. Over the ensuing years, the Eucharist sublated the cowardice of Jesus' disciples into courageous martyrdom as they lived and eventually died as witnesses to Christ. As it did for these once floundering and faltering followers of Jesus, Mark is teaching that the Eucharist can sublate the suffering of the members of his community and their bouts of faltering faith into the strength and courage of Christ, who freely met his death on the cross and emerged victorious.

Cleary then, the words of institution are not solely about what happens to the bread and wine; they are also about what happens to those who willingly and faithfully receive them. During the celebration of the Eucharist, through the transforming power of the Holy Spirit that is invoked within the eucharistic prayer, especially in the epiclesis and the words of institution, bread and wine are sublated into the passion of Christ, or perhaps better, bread and wine become the Christ of the passion. In this sublation of bread and wine into the body and blood of Christ, our own brokenness as human persons and as ordained clergy as well as all the brokenness of God's people is brought into redemptive union with Christ.

Remember that in sublation a lower-order reality is taken up into a higher-order reality and can no longer be identified as it once was—the previously lower-order reality. Now it has become something more. The celebration of the Eucharist is dependent upon a

---

26. See Mark 14:50 and 14:66-72.

whole series of sublations; some of them are radical transformations, others lesser alterations to the nature of something. They begin with what God does in the natural world and they continue with what human effort does, finally leading to what God does with the very elements that human effort has brought forward. Let us take a look at this series of sublations that culminates in the Eucharist and take note of how much "breaking" happens in it (highlighted in italics):

- The eucharistic process of sublation begins with the forces of nature created by God and the labor of farmers whereby seeds that have been planted *die in the ground* and germinate and wheat grows from the earth; the grains of wheat are no longer just seeds or stalks.

- By human labor, wheat is harvested and its grains are *pulverized* to become flour; this flour is no longer a mass of natural grains of wheat but now the necessary component for a staple of food made by humans.

- Next, flour is *mixed* with water to become dough; there is no longer just flour or just water but an indissoluble union for the baking of bread.

- Dough is *kneaded and baked*; the dough has become the edible food of bread.

- In a parallel process, again beginning with the forces of nature created by God and the human labor of vineyard workers who *prune* grape vines, grapes emerge on the vine; they are no longer merely immature leaves on the vine.

- By human labor, grapes are harvested and then *crushed* to extract grape juice; they are no longer a fruit to be eaten but a liquid to be drunk.

- Grape juice is *fermented* to become wine; the juice is chemically "agitated" and becomes a drink of effervescence, no longer merely fruit juice.

- By an act of faith, members of a congregation bring forth bread and wine in the Eucharist **to the deacon and priest** as a symbol of their blessed but *broken* lives; these elements are no longer merely bread and wine for secular use.

- By their ordination, **the deacon and priest** bring the bread and wine to the altar, carrying the *brokenness of God's people and their own* in the bread and wine; this symbol of the lives of God's people now becomes an irrevocable offering to God whereby God is blessed. Never again will these elements return to the sacristy or to the back of the church as merely potential gifts to be brought forward.

- By the power of the Holy Spirit *at work* **in the priest in the midst of the assembly**, the offerings of God's people become the Body and Blood of Christ (*true, real, substantial* presence of Christ as food and drink) that is *broken and poured out*; they are no longer bread and wine nor merely human offerings.

- Those who consume the Body and Blood of Christ are transformed by the Spirit into what they have consumed; they *die to themselves,* no longer just human beings who walk the earth, but now even more potently than before they are the Body and Blood of Christ given for the sake of the world around them.

- Finally, slowly over time, through the eucharistic people, the world is transformed by Christ's presence into the *in-breaking* of the kingdom of God, which is the consummation of the real presence of Christ for all of God's people.

Our ministry as deacons and priests stands right in the middle of the sublation process just outlined, not only liturgically but also spiritually. All the more reason for us to be thoughtful and deliberate about what we do during the Eucharist so that all the more possible we might be claimed by it. Therefore, in order for our role as deacons and priests to be authentic and effective within this series of sublations, we need to allow our own personal brokenness to be sublated into the brokenness of Jesus Christ.

When we take the bread and wine to the altar we need to be aware that our own brokenness is being placed upon the altar; our own anguish and pain are being brought to Christ; our own shattered experience of the church in this moment in the church's history is being offered to God. This is the only way our brokenness becomes generative self-giving to God and to God's people as was Christ's brokenness. It has to be brought into the Eucharist and transformed by the Eucharist. Every time we prepare to celebrate the Eucharist, we need to spend some time in reflection on our own inner passion and ask ourselves:

- How have we painfully experienced the rug being pulled out from underneath us, that what we thought we were getting into in ordained ministry is not what we discovered we have ended up doing?

- How have our wonderful and energizing ideals about diaconate, priesthood, church, or parish life run into the brick wall of reality?

- How have we recognized with some anguish that what motivated us at one time in our diaconal training or seminary formation or earlier years of ordained ministry is not working anymore?

- How have we noticed with some alarm that we are not good at everything in ministry, that we might not even like some aspects of ministry, or that our previous successes and achievements in ministry are not sustaining us in the moment?

- How many weeks, months, years have we felt the grief, anger, and anguish of parishioners who were upset over their parish having to close or merge with another parish, not yet sure ourselves that there were going to be signs of new life in what lay ahead?

- For those who have promised celibacy, how have we felt the torment that all the duties of diaconate or priesthood during the day do not eliminate the periods of loneliness or emptiness at night?

- How has the loss of a loved one, a friend, or a dear parishioner left a gaping hole in our own life?

- How have our own families or personal lives been a source of tremendous pain, or worry, or sense of helplessness?

- How have pangs of guilt haunted us because we made some real blunders in dealing with a person or a group of persons and now it is really difficult to feel authentic at the pulpit or at the altar?

- How are we trapped in our own patterns of sin that make us feel disconnected from Christ?

- How has a voice of shame overtaken us and shattered a sense of the nobility of ordination when we are confronted once again with the awful things that some clergy have done to God's children and God's people?

- How have the shrinking numbers and resources within the parish or diocese made us lose hope or enthusiasm because we end up feeling that we are a part of a diminishing church?

- How have the very real dimensions of our own aging begun to diminish our energy, our enthusiasm, our openness to new ways of thinking or doing things?

These are just some of the forms of our inner passion, that is, the brokenness we experience deep within ourselves due to what is happening within our lives, our ministry, our church. We need to let Christ claim all these things in the Eucharist. We allow Christ to claim them by our own willingness to acknowledge and name them and then deliberately give them over to Christ in our prayer before the Eucharist.

Within the celebration of the Eucharist, the penitential act at the beginning of the liturgy is a good time to name the brokenness we are particularly aware of that day, which needs to be given over to Christ. Deacons can facilitate the effectiveness of the penitential act by allowing what I like to call "the deacon pause." After the presider calls us to a reflective moment at the beginning of the penitential act, the deacon ought not to jump in with the penitential tropes or the Confiteor too soon. The same goes for the presider if no deacon is assisting. I would then call it "the presider's pause." This pause affords us a moment to acknowledge the brokenness that we need Christ to claim, sublate, and redeem in the Eucharist that is about to unfold. If we do not have some "quality time" to acknowledge our own brokenness at the beginning of liturgy, including time internally to name it and surrender it over to Christ, then what unfolds within the rest of the liturgy will be less effective experientially. A hurried pause in the penitential act can too easily lead to a celebration of the liturgy that is less porous, that is, there are fewer openings in our mind, heart, and spirit for the Holy Spirit to claim in us eucharistically what needs to be acknowledged and transformed. This also has the further danger of our receiving Communion in a less-than-recollected fashion, thus diminishing the full meaning of the communion between the eucharistic presence of Christ and our broken personhood, including our lives as deacons and priests.

As already stated, Jesus' presence in the Eucharist can be offered to us precisely because it is broken. Jesus deliberately entered into communion with all human brokenness in his private and public passion. Let us return for a moment to Mark's gospel to also look at Christ's outward or public passion, which begins with his agony in the garden and culminates with his death on the cross. As he sets off to spend some time in prayer in Gethsemane, Jesus experiences the fear of death, saying to his disciples "My soul is sorrowful even to death" (Mark 14:34). He asks the Father to take the cup of suffering from him, the very same cup of suffering he previously asked his disciples if they could drink.[27] And then, upon his arrest, Jesus is betrayed by a friend, abandoned by everyone, spat upon by the Sanhedrin, blindfolded, struck repeatedly, scourged by Pilate's soldiers, and handed over to be crucified. Even on the cross, he is rejected by the other criminals crucified with him, according to Mark.[28] It is on the cross, that Jesus' communion with human brokenness and its inherent sense of alienation reaches its fullness. In union with all those who have suffered greatly and felt abandoned by God in the midst of what they endured, Jesus cries out the words that begin Psalm 22, "My God, my God, why have you forsaken me?" (Mark 15:34). And then he embraces death, the pinnacle of the broken human condition.

In this searing moment of suffering on Calvary, Jesus entered into the depths of human brokenness—all human brokenness in all people of all places and in all moments of history. This is the meaning behind St. Paul saying, "For our sake he made him [Christ] to be sin who did not know sin, so that we might become the righteousness of God in him" (2 Cor 5:21). "Sin," in this instance, refers to the broken human condition from which we need Christ to save us, what we traditionally call "original sin." Christ saves us by entering right into the very depths of the broken human condition. He does not merely look at it, diagnose it, and then declare us free of it. Nor does Jesus merely teach us instructions on how we are to free ourselves from the depths of human sin. In his passion and death, Jesus draws into himself all of our sin, anguish, pain, suffering, and all of the dimensions of the shattered narratives of our lives. In this way Christ claims and redeems all that we really are and all that we have ever been, not merely who we want to be or think we should be.

That redemptive union with Christ is brought to us over and over again in the Eucharist. In the midst of his passion, Jesus made his communion with human brokenness the gift of food and drink

27. See Mark 14:36 and Mark 10:38.
28. Mark 15:32.

that could be ingested in order to be taken into the depths of our own human brokenness. When we consume the Eucharist, our brokenness is sublated into the brokenness of Christ over and over again and thereby allows our own brokenness to become a self-offering to God and nourishment for God's people.

The Eucharist has so many dimensions as the core sacrament of the church. Fundamentally, however, it is the real presence of the dying and rising Christ who is food and drink for us. Therefore, to consume the body of Christ is to consume his constant dying for us, with us, and in us. In every Eucharist, we eat Christ's dying and take it into our deepest core where it consecrates our every form of dying-to-self that needs to happen in us throughout our lives, sometimes painfully. Likewise, to drink in the blood of Christ is to slake in the constant self-emptying of Christ on the cross that now seeps into our blood stream and sanctifies every self-emptying demanded by our ordination and summoned by our ministry. In all of this, our personal narratives as deacons and priests become a eucharistic proclamation of the death of the Lord.

However, as noted earlier in this chapter, though the Eucharist is always a meal of Christ's death and communion with human brokenness, it is also a sumptuous feast of Christ's life and his presence as God's love which heals and redeems our broken human condition. Therefore, to take and eat the body of Christ is to reach for new life. The body of Christ is the fully alive Christ who abundantly feeds us all that God is for us so that we can become fully alive. To consume the Eucharist is to consume every aspect of the identity of Jesus Christ, every moment of his ministry that brought healing, mercy, and transformation to the world so that the world might come alive with all that Christ offers. Furthermore, to take and drink the blood of Christ is to come to fuller life because the love of Christ now pulsates through our veins. The blood of Christ stimulates our own capacity for love, since in the Eucharist we drink in the love of Christ that was poured out in his blood from the cross to become the drink that gives true life.

All of this is to say that, for priests and deacons, the Eucharist is vital to how the Holy Spirit lays an *ontological claim* on us and leads us into becoming one with the risen Christ, who is the true and everlasting servant and priest. It is Christ's Spirit who enacts the Eucharist that now makes us through the Eucharist into the deacons and priests we are called to be. But it all happens slowly—over time—with every deliberate and faith-filled communion between our brokenness and the brokenness of Christ, which in turn brings us communion with the life that Christ gives to us. Inherently, then, our eucharistic communion with Christ in brokenness leads to our eucharistic oneness with Christ in self-giving to God and to God's people. "To break" becomes "to give." This we will explore in the next chapter.

Prayer and Reflection

Take a few moments of silent reflection.
Prayerfully ponder the following:

1. Ask the Holy Spirit to unite you to Christ as he walks the Way to Calvary.

2. What are some experiences of your own private passion that you carry inside of you?
   - Image Jesus meeting you on the path and asking you to give him your private passion.
   - Image Jesus reaching out his hand and taking those experiences from your heart and placing them inside of his.
   - What is he asking you to take from him?

3. What are some of the experiences of public passion that your community or members of your community are currently enduring?
   - Who has lost loved ones?
   - Who has lost a job or endured a public scandal?
   - What families are enduring a difficult crisis?
   - What aspects of being a vibrant community of faith are floundering or dying in your place of ministry?

4. Image Jesus taking all of that into his heart as he walks toward Calvary.
   - What does he want your community to take from him?

5. Pray the *Anima Christi*.
   Soul of Christ, sanctify me.
   Body of Christ, save me.
   Blood of Christ, embolden me.
   Water from the side of Christ, wash me.
   Passion of Christ, strengthen me.
   O good Jesus, hear me.
   Within your wounds hide me.
   Never permit me to be parted from you.
   From the evil Enemy defend me.
   At the hour of my death call me
   and bid me come to you,
   that with your Saints I may praise you
   for age upon age.
   Amen.

chapter six

GIVE

*For God so loved the world that he gave his only Son,
so that everyone who believes in him might not perish
but might have eternal life.*

—John 3:16

I t is commonplace for us to speak about giving presents to
one another, giving advice and counsel to those who need
it, giving a donation to a worthy cause, and giving our place
in line to someone who needs it more than we do. In addition,
lovers speak of giving their hearts to their beloved; motivational
speakers rouse their audience's desire to give their all to the goals
they want to achieve; and coaches demand that their teams give
110 percent to winning the game. In another sense, a person can
say "I give," indicating that one is "bending" to the will of another
or surrendering one's own intransigence in order to reach some
sort of agreement with others during an impasse in a common
pursuit. In all of these different connotations of what it means "to
give," there is an underlying subtext that unifies them—*to empty
oneself for the sake of the other*, which is the very meaning of the
biblical concept of *kenosis*. Even more, in all the different ways
that our giving is *kenosis,* we are offering to others our very selves
in varying degrees of intensity. Some aspect of who we are—our
heart, mind, will, or inner life—is offered whenever we give to

others something that we have within ourselves or something that comes from the resources of our lives.

It should come as no surprise then that Jesus is the very archetype of *kenosis*.[1] In every instance of Jesus' giving, there is his grace-filled self-emptying, that is, the offer of his very self. When Jesus dines with his disciples on the night before his death, he gives to them bread and wine, declaring them to be his body and blood, meaning his entire personhood and life's energy. But this eucharistic moment of Jesus "giving" himself occurs within an entire narrative of the self-giving of God in the incarnation Christ, as this chapter's opening quote from John's gospel captures. The very giving of Jesus' body and blood, which unfolds within his final meal with the disciples and culminates in his death, occurs within the "giving" of God's love that has been taking place throughout the life story of the Son of God in the flesh.

Let us recap this story that is to claim our own stories. First of all, Jesus "takes" on human flesh (the life he receives from the Father through the Spirit). In this "taking," there is always within Jesus an awareness of his intimacy with the Father in everything that he experiences. Secondly, this awareness allows Jesus, in gratitude, to "bless" God through his incarnate life of self-emptying love for God and for God's people. Thirdly, this self-emptying life of Jesus reaches its climax when he is "broken" in a self-sacrificing death by which Jesus draws all human brokenness into redemptive communion with God's saving love. Therefore, the "breaking" of Jesus is inherently the "giving" of God's very self in love to the world, which becomes the crucial and definitive piece within the plotline of the eucharistic story of Christ. As outlined above, the redemptive narrative of the Son of God demonstrates that the entirety of Christ's life of "taking," "blessing," and "breaking" becomes sublated by God's love into "giving." The Eucharist is the sacrament of this entire sacred narrative, ritually and spiritually drawing us ever more fully into that story line.

---

1. See the discussion of *kenosis* in chap. 4.

In the eucharistic narrative that the church ritualizes in the liturgy, we take, bless, and break bread (and pour wine), and then receive them as the broken body and poured out blood of Christ given in love for the salvation of the world. In the life of the church, the Eucharist originates from Christ who commands his disciples to take and eat his body and drink his blood that is given for them and for the many, that is, for the life of the world. What originates sacramentally in this giving of Christ leads liturgically to the same giving *to us* as participants in the Eucharist; furthermore, liturgically, it ends with the same giving *by us* to the many, that is, to all of God's beloved people. As deacons and priests, we need to embody with a *magnetic density* this eucharistic giving of Christ as God's love for the world. It is to be *magnetic* in that it is to draw the people we serve into doing the very same in their lives. This magnetism demands that our eucharistic giving have some *density* in the sense that there needs to be a substantial and manifest authenticity in how the Eucharist has claimed us. Only with this *magnetic density* can we, as deacons and priests at the end of liturgy, bless and send our people into the same eucharistic giving they are to offer to the larger world. Without evidencing that we have been claimed by the Eucharist ourselves we cannot effectively "mission" our people into the *magnetic density* that they are to evidence in their daily lives by their own participation in the Liturgy of the Eucharist.

Our personal narratives, claimed by the eucharistic liturgy we celebrate so often, ought to be sublated into the self-giving of God's love to the people we serve. The Eucharist transforms us into persons who, in giving all that Christ is for us, give to God's people all that we have become in Christ. In turn, this is to energize our people into doing the same in all of the concrete circumstances of their lives. As ordinary ministers of the Eucharist, we deacons and priests cannot repeatedly celebrate the Eucharist and yet resist or ignore this powerful, beautiful, and grace-filled process of sublation. The authenticity of our diaconate and priesthood depends on this; so too does our effectiveness, which arises from our willingness to let the Holy Spirit join our brokenness to Christ's so that Christ's self-giving to human brokenness becomes our credible and grace-filled self-giving to the brokenness of the lives of the people we serve and to the world in which we live.

There is a chain of theological and sacramental statements of faith that is important for us to grasp because it helps us understand how our eucharistic narrative moves from "breaking" to "giving." It goes like this:

1. The body of Christ is the Bread of Life come down from heaven to be eaten, digested, and absorbed into ourselves so that we become what we eat. We become the body of Christ for the world.

2. The body of Christ is *broken*, precisely so that it can become food for us.

3. The blood of Christ is the wine of salvation—the very life force of Christ who is God's unconditional and merciful love that transforms everyone and everything.

4. This blood of Christ—the life force of Christ as Love—is *poured* precisely so that it can be slaked in, swallowed, digested, and absorbed into our very core so that we become what we drink. We become the blood of Christ for the world.

5. Therefore, the very *breaking* during the Eucharist is inherently connected to the very self-giving that occurs within the Eucharist. This is deeply embedded within the true, real, and substantial nature of the real presence of Christ, as we have already seen.

6. The broken and poured out Christ is the real presence of Christ in his *kenosis* (complete self-giving in love) that is most fully manifested in his dying for us, in which he assumes all human brokenness into himself. Thus, in the broken and poured out Christ on the cross and in the Eucharist all human brokenness is sublated into self-giving in love.

7. Through the Holy Spirit we are configured to Christ's self-giving in love by our ordination, and that configuration is

nourished, strengthened, and deepened through the Eucharist. In turn, through our liturgical roles as deacons and priests, the Eucharist missions us to nourish, strengthen, and deepen our people's configuration to the same self-giving of Christ that the Holy Spirit effected in their baptism and confirmation.

Keep in mind that the eucharistic narrative of Christ is never merely about who Christ is in and of himself; it is always about who Christ is *for us and for the many*. Therefore, when we consume the Eucharist, the communion of our brokenness with Christ's is not the ultimate goal of the sacramental celebration. It is never merely a "me-and-Jesus" moment; something we warn our people about all the time. Instead, our communion-in-brokenness is to be sublated into Christ's self-giving over and over again, thereby allowing our own brokenness to become a self-offering to God and to God's people. The Eucharist teaches priests and deacons that we can never minister to God's people apart from our own brokenness-with-Christ. There is no "giving" that is disconnected from the "breaking." What might this entail within our own spiritual lives and ministry?

- Our own awareness of the mercy we have received for our sins is to become a merciful engagement with others struggling with their sinfulness.

- Our recognition that our own families and circles of friends are flawed—perhaps even dysfunctional—but infinitely loved by Christ is to become patience and insight in helping others deal with their own broken families and friends.

- Our own struggles with shame, failure, resentment, jealousy, pride, estrangement, or greed are to become wisdom and understanding with those who struggle with the same things.

- Our own inner anguish over the brokenness in the church that can no longer be denied is to become resolute forbearance to stand by those who struggle with the church and an equally resolute determination to reach out to and hold in prayer those who have walked away from the church.

- Our own experiences of grief, sadness, disappointment, illness and pain, in which we have found deeper intimacy with the passion of Christ, are to become life-giving compassion for those experiencing their own forms of suffering.

Recall from the previous chapter how in the words of institution in Mark's gospel Jesus refers to the cup of his blood as "being shed for the many." Jesus' blood is not merely shed; it is *shed for* all who long to be saved from the broken human condition. We saw how this revealed that Jesus' passion—his embracing of human brokenness—becomes self-giving. In other words, in the *breaking* of Jesus is the *giving* of Jesus. In commenting on the passion, theologian Glenn Ambrose writes that Jesus' death "only confirms his commitment to live a life of giving."[2] In the words of noted French sacramentologist Louis-Marie Chauvet, Jesus' "dying-for is the ultimate expression of his living-for."[3] This archetypal *kenosis* of Jesus means that, for any who are configured to Christ by baptism-confirmation and by holy orders, there is no giving of self without embracing being broken selves united to Christ in that brokenness. Our own breaking becomes the means of our giving.

"*Breaking* Us" into Deacons and Priests to Be *Given* to God's People

It would be wonderful if our people in the pews, as well as those who no longer sit there, could grasp this concept that connects so intimately who they are with all that Christ is for them, as well

---

2. Glenn P. Ambrose, *The Theology of Louis-Marie Chauvet: Overcoming Onto-Theology with the Sacramental Tradition* (New York: Routledge, 2016), 145.

3. Louis-Marie Chauvet, *Symbol and Sacrament: Sacramental Reinterpretation of Christian Existence,* trans. Madeleine Beaumont and Patrick Madigan (Collegeville, MN: Liturgical Press, 1995), 298.

as joins the stuff of their lives with the substance of the Eucharist. That is precisely where we priests and deacons come in. But in order for us to effect this understanding in the people we serve, we need to grasp it firmly within ourselves. To understand the eucharistic "giving" dimension of the roles into which we were ordained, let us return to the rites of ordination.

Recall what we examined in part 1 of this book: After the moment of election, when the candidates for ordination to the diaconate are called forth and the bishop and church have approved them, the bishop asks a series of questions of the elect. One of those questions is: "Do you resolve to *conform your way of life* always to the example of Christ, of whose Body and Blood you are ministers at the altar?"[4] An affirmative response to this question is actually assent to allowing one's way of life to be sublated into the body and blood of Christ. How does this happen in a man being ordained a deacon?

In the prayer of ordination for deacons, the bishop prays:

> Send forth upon them, O Lord, we pray,
> the Holy Spirit,
> that they may be strengthened by the gift of your sevenfold
> grace for the faithful carrying out of the work of the ministry.
>
> May they abound in every Gospel virtue:
> unfeigned love, concern for the sick and the poor,
> unassuming authority, the purity of innocence,
> and the observance of spiritual discipline.
>
> May your commandments shine forth in their conduct,
> so that by the example of their way of life
> they may inspire the imitation of your holy people . . . (207)

The prayer of ordination reveals that deacons are: (1) to be open and attentive constantly to the stirrings and movement of the Holy Spirit within them and within their lives (i.e., men of discernment);

---

4. *Rites of Ordination*, 200.

(2) to be claimed by the gospel in their own way of life since the gospel is Christ; (3) to live concretely Christ's way of life as a genuinely loving servant to the sick and poor; (4) to minister with humility and an undivided heart; (5) to be intent about the deepening of their spiritual lives; (6) to be a vivid and captivating example of what it means to live the Way of Christ; (7) to draw others into the Way of Christ.

Similarly, as we saw in part 1, near the conclusion of the rite of ordination of priests, the bishop receives the bread and wine from the people and then presents them to the newly ordained priests. He says to them: "Receive the oblation of the holy people, to be offered to God. Understand what you do, imitate what you celebrate, and *conform your life* to the mystery of the Lord's cross" (135). How does a man become a priest whose life has been sublated into the oblation of the holy people and the mystery of the Lord's cross?

In the prayer of ordination for priests, the bishop prays:

> Almighty Father . . .
> renew deep within them the Spirit of holiness . . .
> and by the example of their manner of life,
> may they instill right conduct.
>
> May they be worthy coworkers with our Order,
> so that by their preaching
> and through the grace of the Holy Spirit
> the words of the Gospel may bear fruit in human hearts
> and reach even to the ends of the earth.
>
> Together with us, may they be faithful stewards of your mysteries,
> so that your people may be renewed in the waters of rebirth
> and nourished from your altar;
> so that sinners may be reconciled and the sick raised up.
> May they be joined with us, Lord,
> in imploring your mercy for the people entrusted to their care
> and for all the world. (131)

The prayer of ordination declares that priests are: (1) to be open and attentive constantly to how the Spirit is calling them to deeper holiness; (2) to live lives of moral uprightness that captivate and inspire others to do the same; (3) to be men of communion with their bishop and, therefore, the larger church; (4) to be claimed by the Word of God in such a way that they preach effectively; (5) to evangelize the larger world beyond the pews; (6) to prayerfully and deliberately celebrate the sacraments; (7) to claim sacramentally every aspect of people's lives from birth to death for Christ; (8) to intercede in prayer constantly for those in need of God's mercy and for the larger world.

The rites of ordination spell out very clearly and specifically what we are to "give" to God's people as deacons and priests. By allowing the Eucharist to claim us ever more fully and sublate us ever more deeply into Christ as deacon and Christ as priest, we can then be more attuned to what that transformation evokes from us, what it draws out from us, what it enables and demands that we give in and through our ministries animated by the Eucharist.

First of all, we need to teach people the meaning of the celebration of the Eucharist in a way that allows them to recognize the deep connections among experiencing the *haecceitas* of their own broken lives, the offering of bread and wine within the liturgy, and the receiving of the body and blood of Christ. Subsequently, we need to help them experience these deep connections as empowerment for their missioning out into the world at the end of the liturgy. The seminarians I teach hear me repeatedly insist within any course I offer that one of the greatest needs in parish life today is adult faith formation. More specifically, perhaps there is no greater urgency in our parishes, where the number of those participating in the Eucharist regularly is shrinking, than to help adults grasp the deeper layers and meaning of the Liturgy of the Eucharist, especially as it connects to their own lives, their own struggles and confusion, their own hopes and dreams, their own responsibilities as Christian women and men.

Secondly, we need to proclaim and preach the Word of God in a way that draws people into the flow of sublation that is happening throughout the Eucharist. For this to happen, we fundamentally have to be claimed each day by the Word of God we are ordained to proclaim and preach. Etched within our hearts and minds needs to be this truism: *we cannot captivate* **others** *with what does not claim* **us**! Pope Francis takes this point very seriously. In his apostolic exhortation *Evangelii Gaudium*, he states: "When preaching takes place within the context of the liturgy, it is part of the offering made to the Father and a mediation of the grace which Christ pours out during the celebration. This context demands that preaching should guide the assembly, and the preacher, to a life-changing communion with Christ in the Eucharist" (138). For this to happen, the pope (quoting Pope Paul VI's *Evangelii Nuntiandi*) reminds preachers of the Word that: "Today . . . people prefer to listen to witnesses: they 'thirst for authenticity' and 'call for evangelizers to speak of a God whom they themselves know and are familiar with, as if they were seeing him' " (150).

As authentic witnesses to the gospel, priests and deacons need to help their people to be claimed by the Word through the three-year lectionary cycle of readings. Through the entire selection of readings it becomes clear how Christ is intimately joined to everything our people are experiencing in their lives, everything they endure, everything they struggle with, everything they fail at, and everything for which they truly long. Then ordained preachers ought to help God's people discover how Christ is seeking to grace and transform each experience and every element of their lives into intimacy with Christ.

Preachers ought to spell out how the Word of God is calling for transformations within each person, among the members of the community, and within the world, *as that Word has first called for transformations in the ones who are preaching.* We deacons and priests cannot insist that others struggle with a conversion we have not yet allowed to begin in us. We ought to offer guidance in how the Scripture readings can help to deepen one's interior life and sanctify one's day-to-day living, which means we need to let the Scriptures deepen our own interior life and claim every part of our day-to-day living.

Thirdly, we need to live the eucharistic way of life in a captivating way that draws *others* to what animates *us*. Deacons in their workplaces, families, social circles, and places of ministry need to live vividly the Way of Christ so that others are attracted to it and then seek the source of nourishment and strength for living the Way of Christ themselves. Furthermore, deacons need to embody with gusto the service to the poor (and the marginalized) that all the baptized are called to offer and, thereby, animate others in joining in concrete service to the poor (and the marginalized).

In a similar vein, priests need to demonstrate in their interactions with parishioners, staff, other clergy, the bishop, and the public the nature of being a "man of communion."[5] In this way, transformed by eucharistic communion, the priest can lead his people in transforming into unitive energy the toxic energy of divisiveness that has poisoned our society's public discourse and the nature of interactions within our culture and even within our church. In the epiclesis over the people in the Eucharistic Prayer for Reconciliation I, the priest prays:

> Look kindly, most compassionate Father, on those you unite to yourself by the Sacrifice of your Son, and grant that, by the power of the Holy Spirit, as they partake of this one Bread and one Chalice, they may be gathered into one Body in Christ, who heals every division.

In the Eucharistic Prayer for Various Needs I, the following is prayed right after the epiclesis over the people:

> Lord, renew your Church by the light of the Gospel. Strengthen the bond of unity between the faithful and the pastors of your people, together with N. our Pope, N. our Bishop, and the whole Order of Bishops, that in a world torn by strife your people may shine forth as a prophetic sign of unity and concord.

To pray these words authentically, the priest must live genuinely the virtue of building communion in the church and in the world.

---

5. Pope John Paul II, *Pastores Dabo Vobis,* Post-Synodal Apostolic Exhortation, 43.

Furthermore, priests need to embody with *magnetic density* the life of virtue that all the baptized are called to live and, thereby, "instill right conduct" (as prayed in the rite of ordination) in others by what we live and not only by what we teach or admonish others to live. Notice the moral imperatives toward virtue that are contained within the second half of different eucharistic prayers. They make clear "the right conduct" that the Eucharist is to "instill" in us:

- "Remember, Lord, your Church, spread throughout the world, and bring her to the fullness of charity . . ." (Eucharistic Prayer II).

- "And so, having called us to your table, Lord, confirm us in unity, so that together with N. our Pope and N. our Bishop, with all Bishops, Priests, and Deacons, and your entire people, as we walk your ways with faith and hope, we may strive to bring joy and trust into the world . . ." (Eucharistic Prayer for Various Needs II).

- "Keep us attentive to the needs of all that, sharing their grief and pain, their joy and hope, we may faithfully bring them the good news of salvation and go forward with them along the way of your Kingdom . . ." (Eucharistic Prayer for Various Needs III).

- "Open our eyes to the needs of our brothers and sisters; inspire in us words and actions to comfort those who labor and are burdened. Make us serve them truly, after the example of Christ and at his command. And may your Church stand as a living witness to truth and freedom, to peace and justice, that all people may be raised up to a new hope."

What all of this boils down to is that, as ordinary ministers of the Eucharist, the liturgical role of priests and deacons does not culminate in merely giving Holy Communion to God's people, as if that moment were the fulfillment and completion of "giving" within the eucharistic narrative. When we reduce eucharistic "giving" merely to the distribution of Holy Communion, we have forgotten that the Eucharist is an encounter with the person of Christ whose eucharistic narrative claims our whole lives. We end up relegating "giving" to the mere reception of a sacred reality that our people might receive with reverence but then often dismiss with diligence. In other words, the Eucharist makes no claim on them either.

What we are to give our people in the Eucharist is so much more. In and through the liturgy, ordained clerics are called to give to our people a vibrant, authentic, captivating, challenging, comforting, and joyful witness to what it means to be claimed by the eucharistic story of Christ that we celebrate. In the second epiclesis of the Eucharistic Prayer for Various Needs III, the priest prays:

> By our partaking of this mystery, almighty Father, give us life through your Spirit, grant that we may be conformed to the image of your Son, confirm us in the bond of communion, together with N. our Pope and N. our Bishop, with all other Bishops, with Priests and Deacons, and with your entire people.

At a time in the church when so many people are walking away from the Eucharist—some even choosing to go to other Christian churches that are very non-eucharistic or very low-eucharistic— our people need to see that the eucharistic narrative has grabbed hold of us, made a difference in who we are and what we do, and transformed how we live. If *our* lives are not sublated into the living presence of Christ by the Eucharist, how can we ever expect to lead others into the Christic transformation that the Eucharist seeks to bring to *their* lives?

What we teach, proclaim, and live as deacons and priests are all part of the self-emptying within ministry to which we are called. As already stated, this self-emptying "breaks" us. It breaks open our hearts and minds. It breaks apart our resistance to ongoing conversion. It shatters our ego's need for reward and recognition for our ministry. It pierces into our deepest self. When we allow our brokenness to be joined experientially and spiritually to Christ's broken body and poured out blood in the Eucharist, we are then given and poured out to God's people as ordained men who have truly been *ontologically claimed* and transformed into Christ the deacon and Christ the priest *for them*. They will find in us the way that sanctifies their own brokenness. They will learn from us how to allow their sacred brokenness to become generative of Christ's presence for others. They will see in us the icon of the self-emptying of Christ, which, they recognize deep down, is what they want to live within the particularities of their own lives.

Hopefully, our own authentic embodiment of *giving* will allow our ministry among the people of God to be eucharistic at all times, inviting our people to seek out from us the tangibility of Christ's presence within their lives in a way that connects with the tangibility of Christ's presence that they experience within the Eucharist. They would witness in us the slow—ever so slow—process of sublation, in which the Holy Spirit, who ontologically claimed them on the day of their baptism and even further on the day of their confirmation, is constantly at work in them bringing to fulfillment all they are meant to be as the body and blood of Christ in the world. The Eucharist nourishes them for this very task, which is why the liturgy ends with the sending forth.

"Giving" as Sending

It is still common parlance to speak of the Liturgy of the Eucharist as "the Mass." As we know, the word "Mass" comes from the formula for the sending forth at the end of the Latin liturgy, "*Ite, missa est.*" These words were often translated as "Go, the Mass is ended;" however, the phrase can literally be translated as "Go, it is the dismissal." In commenting on this, John Baldovin writes: "The fact that the Mass takes one of its most important names from the dismissal is worthy of some reflection. In a sense, the Eucharist does not exist merely for itself but rather for our becoming the Body of Christ, both individually and corporately in our daily lives."[6] Therefore, let us not be dismissive of the dismissal; there is tremendous meaning and value to the concluding rites of the eucharistic liturgy. They constitute a significant portion of the "giving" in the eucharistic narrative. The *General Instruction of the Roman Missal* says that the concluding rites consist of the "dismissal of the people by the deacon or the priest, so that each may go out and do good works, praising and blessing God" (90).

A dismissal is actually a "sending." Within the narrative of the Eucharist, the dismissal proclaims that the whole point of the celebration of the Eucharist is to send all participants out into the world to live what they have celebrated. As the gospels end with the risen Christ sending the disciples out into the world to do as he did, so too does the liturgy of Christ's presence send all of us to continue the mission of Christ as the living presence of Christ in the world. It is essential that this notion of "sending" be grasped so that participants within the liturgy do not become mere "consumers." The Mass was never about "getting the goods one came for," for example, receiving Communion and then getting back to one's life. The Mass is a powerfully sacramental experience of the sublation of our lives into the body and blood of Christ, who is the very sending of the Father's love into the world. Therefore, as we become what we eat and drink, we who participate in the Eucharist become the presence of Christ sent into the world to embody the love of God. The Mass is never about "what we get;" it is always about "what we give" because of who we become.

The liturgical roles of deacon and priest are conjoined within the "sending" of the people at the end of liturgy. The priest evokes the continued presence of Emmanuel in the lives of the participants when he says "The Lord be with you." On more solemn occasions, the deacon then invites the people to "bow down for the blessing." The priest subsequently prays over the people and blesses them, upon which the deacon then sends them forth. The

6. John F. Baldovin, SJ, *Bread of Life, Cup of Salvation: Understanding the Mass* (Lanham, MD: Rowman & Littlefield, 2003), 149.

most illustrative dismissals that capture the meaning of being sent forth are: "Go and announce the Gospel of the Lord" and "Go in peace, glorifying the Lord by your life."[7]

The "Amen" by the people expresses their consent to be sent and give glory to God in the way they live. It voices their willingness to be claimed by the final element of the eucharistic narrative of Christ—"to give." But do they know this? Evoking the scenes of the risen Christ appearing to Mary Magdalene and the two disciples on the road to Emmaus who then went off and shared with others what they experienced, Henri Nouwen writes:

> Communion is not the end. Mission is. Communion, that sacred intimacy with God, is not the final moment of the Eucharistic life. We recognized him, but that recognition is not just for us to savor or to keep a secret. As Mary of Magdala, so too the two friends had heard deep within themselves the words "Go and tell." That's the conclusion of the Eucharistic celebration: that too is the final call of the Eucharistic life. "Go and tell. What you have heard and seen is not just for yourself. It is for the brothers and sisters and for all who are ready to receive it. Go, don't linger, don't wait, don't hesitate, but move now and return to the places from which you came, and let those you left behind in their hiding places know that there is nothing to be afraid of, that he is risen, risen indeed."[8]

Nouwen continues that, as we are sent out, the mission unites us together. He states:

> The Eucharist is always mission. The Eucharist that has freed us from the paralyzing sense of loss and revealed to us that the Spirit of Jesus lives within us and empowers us to go out into the world and bring good news to the poor, sight to the blind,

---

7. *The Roman Missal,* see 141 and 144.

8. Henri J. M. Nouwen, *With Burning Hearts: A Meditation on the Eucharistic Life* (Maryknoll, NY: Orbis Books, 1994), 103–4.

liberty to the captives, and to proclaim that God has shown again his favor to all people. But we are not sent out alone; we are sent with our brothers and sisters who also know that Jesus lives within them.[9]

The role of the deacon and priest within the life of the parish is to help people grasp this key dimension of the Eucharist. However, for that to happen, there does not necessarily need to be liturgical renewal within the community, but a more vibrant sense of the person of Jesus Christ. Sacramental theologian Kenan Osborne, warns that if the celebration of the Eucharist within a community suffers "from a certain kind of inertia, the major issue cannot be on making the liturgy more exciting . . . [but rather] it should be focused on making Jesus more exciting."[10] This will help ensure that every eucharistic community is an assembly of members from, what Osborne calls, a "Jesus community." He describes what that looks like:

> A Jesus community is not simply a community that thinks alike. It is an action-oriented community, not an ideology-oriented community. In other words, the eucharistic community *strives* (action) to be Christlike, *follows* (action) the impulse of the Holy Spirit, and leaves the table (action) to bring the meaning of the Eucharist to daily life.[11]

What this implies is that the very sending at the end of liturgy defines the whole point of gathering for liturgy in the first place. The "giving" that completes the eucharistic narrative fulfills the meaning of the "taking," "blessing," and "breaking" that have preceded it. Therefore, before the priest and deacon can effectively send the congregation in the concluding rites, they need to help form the

9. Nouwen, 111–12.

10. Kenan B. Osborne, OFM, *Community, Eucharist, and Spirituality* (Liguori, MO: Liguori Publications, 2007), 17.

11. Osborne, 26.

congregation's understanding of the person of Jesus Christ before the liturgy even begins and throughout the liturgy. The priest and deacon need to become expert "Christologians" on behalf of the people they serve.

If, at the conclusion of every eucharistic celebration, we keep sending our people out into the world to be the presence of Christ, then it is incumbent upon us to guide them well in their journey of coming to know Christ intimately. To do this, we have to know Christ intimately ourselves. This happens on intellectual and conceptual levels in the Christology classes we take during our years of initial diaconal and priestly formation; but it also needs to continue long after ordination through the reading and studying of good sources on Christology. More importantly, however, the process of our becoming good Christologians for the sake of our people has to happen on a personal and spiritual level deep within our prayer lives and within our faith-filled pondering of the people we encounter, the events that unfold, and the experiences we have in our day-to-day living. This allows us to give to our people the fruits of our own relationship to Christ that is nourished by our prayer.

"*Giving*" as Offering Prayer and Praise to God

In the end, the quality and authenticity of the exercise of our liturgical roles as deacons and priests within the Eucharist come from the depth and substance of our personal relationship to Jesus Christ before, during, and after the eucharistic celebration. If the Eucharist is our entering into the narrative of Christ, including entering into Christ's self-sacrifice of praise and thanksgiving to the Father, then we need to know Christ and what it "feels" like to be in Christ who is in us. In the rite of ordination of deacons, as he prays over those on whom he has just laid hands, the bishop invokes the Holy Spirit so that the deacons "may remain strong and steadfast in Christ" (207). At the ordination of priests, the bishop asks the candidates, "Do you resolve to be united more closely every day to Christ the High Priest, who offered himself for us to the Father as a pure sacrifice, and with him to consecrate yourselves to God for the salvation of all?" (124). The ordination ritual summons both deacons and priests not merely to imitate Christ or know Christ but to give themselves over to being drawn into Christ's very personhood as both eternal servant and priest for the people of God. This necessitates our giving time to Christ in prayer because prayer is the quintessential form of exchange that allows us not only to know Christ intimately but to be drawn into Christ mystically, spiritually, and experientially.

Being in Christ means being within the eternal self-offering in love and praise that he gives to the Father. It is an existential state of endless "giving" of ourselves in Christ to the God who created us and claimed us, which means, at the same time, a constant giving of ourselves in Christ to God's people. This allows us to see that the eucharistic narrative of Jesus is not linear, but cyclic. What begins with the Father's self-giving in love for the world through the incarnation of Jesus ends with giving praise to the Father through the Eucharist of Christ who has gathered all of us into himself. This is the christological *exitio-reditio* dynamic of the incarnation and paschal mystery that scholars see most vividly portrayed in the Gospel of John. In this dynamic, God gives of himself (empties himself into the world) in the person of Jesus who becomes incarnate for all of us (the *exitio* movement of Christ). This reaches its fullness in Christ's embrace of human brokenness, even unto death.[12] The death of Jesus is also the beginning of the *reditio* movement of Christ who returns to the Father when he is lifted up on the cross in glory and draws all people to himself.[13] The entire *exitio-reditio* movement of Christ is framed by "giving," more specifically "self-giving." The eucharistic narrative captures this entire movement and brings us into communion with it over and over again.

While all of God's people are drawn into this cyclic narrative, as deacons and priests we need to accompany them and lead them

---

12. See the prologue of John's gospel (1:1-18) for the clearest expression of the *exitio* of Christ.

13. See John 12:32; 13:3; 14:6; 17:20-26 for the key passages that capture the *reditio* movement of the incarnation and paschal mystery.

effectively in the *exitio-reditio* narrative of Christ by entering into it vividly, wholeheartedly, and constantly in our own prayer lives. Our eucharistic communion with Christ's self-giving in praise to the Father and in service to God's people is given vigor and vitality through all the forms of personal prayer we might engage in, but in a special way through our communion with Christ that occurs in the Liturgy of the Hours. In the Constitution on the Sacred Liturgy, the link between the Eucharist and the Liturgy of the Hours through the *exitio-reditio* of Christ is made clear:

> Jesus Christ, high priest of the new and eternal covenant, taking human nature, introduced into this earthly exile that hymn which is sung throughout all ages in the realms above. He joins the entire community of humankind to himself, associating it with himself in singing his divine song of praise.
>
> For it is through his church itself that he continues this priestly work. The church, by celebrating the Eucharist and in other ways, especially the celebration of the divine office, is ceaselessly engaged in praising the Lord and interceding for the salvation of the entire world. (*Sacrosanctum Concilium*, 83)

The Liturgy of the Hours habituates in those who pray it an awareness of all that God has given to us, most fully in Christ, and a desire to enter into Christ's praise and thanksgiving to the Father. This fosters a greater capacity to "take" our lives, our parish, our church, our world as graced gifts of God to us, which, in turn, engenders in us a greater ability to "bless" God in our ministry as deacons and priests. Furthermore, the psalms of lament that we constantly pray within the Divine Office generate a deeper awareness that all human brokenness is given to God and enters the heart of Christ, who is broken for all. Finally, praying the Divine Office instills in us a deeper desire and capacity in our hearts, minds, and wills to be drawn into the self-emptying (the self-giving) love of Christ for God's people that praises the Father. As you can see, the plotline of the eucharistic narrative (take, bless, break, give) permeates what we celebrate in the Liturgy of the

Hours. Even more, the Liturgy of the Hours "is in turn an excellent preparation for the celebration of the eucharist itself, for it inspires and deepens in a fitting way the dispositions necessary for the fruitful celebration of the eucharist: faith, hope, love, devotion, and the spirit of self-denial."[14]

All ordained clerics pledged to praying the Liturgy of the Hours when we were ordained deacons. After the election of the candidates, the bishop asked: "Do you resolve to maintain and deepen the spirit of prayer that is proper to your way of life and, in keeping with the spirit and what is required of you, to celebrate faithfully the Liturgy of the Hours with and for the People of God and indeed for the whole world?"[15] Our "I do" to that question was a pledge of constantly giving ourselves over to the prayer of Christ. The repeated recitation of psalms and canticles throughout the day makes tangible in time our communion with Christ's timeless praise of the Father. Furthermore, our "I do" was the promise to give our people and the whole world prayerfully and mindfully to God in union with Christ. In our prayer, as in our ministry, we tether the lives of others to the tender mercy of our God in, with, and through Christ. Praying the Divine Office is a powerfully grace-filled way that the Holy Spirit, throughout the day, sublates us more and more into the eucharistic Christ, who is the very "giving" of God's self to us. At the same time, praying the Divine Office is the Spirit at work in us claiming more and more of who we are and what we live, thereby drawing our lives more fully into Christ's priestly "self-giving" in praise and thanksgiving to God and Christ's redemptive "self-giving" to God's people and the whole of creation.

Admittedly, the Liturgy of the Hours is not the exclusive prayer of ordained clerics. The *General Instruction of the Liturgy of the Hours* (*GILOH*) even calls for the greater promotion of its celebration by the whole priestly people of God. It states: "The liturgy

14. Congregation for Divine Worship, *General Instruction of the Liturgy of the Hours* (1971), 12.

15. *Rites of Ordination*, 200.

of the hours, like other liturgical services, is not a private matter but belongs to the whole Body of the Church, whose life it both expresses and affects" (20). The *GILOH* even goes so far as to assert that "whenever it is possible to have a celebration in common, with the people present and actively taking part, this kind of celebration is preferred to one that is individual and, as it were, private" (33). Hence, the document charges deacons and priests with the special responsibility of inviting their people to celebrate the Liturgy of the Hours with them, "and prepared by suitable instruction, to celebrate principal hours in common, especially on Sundays and holydays" (22). Notice the call for the people to participate in the Divine Office especially on the very same days that they would most often participate in the Eucharist as well. Furthermore, the *GILOH* says that deacons and priests "should teach the people how to make this participation a source of genuine prayer; they should therefore give the people suitable guidance in the Christian understanding of the psalms, in order to progress by degrees to a greater appreciation and more frequent use of the prayer of the Church" (23). Just as the Eucharist is a communal prayer in which all the gathered people of God participate in the eucharistic narrative of Christ, so too the Liturgy of the Hours is meant to be a communal prayer that extends and savors the Eucharist, thus allowing that eucharistic narrative of Christ to permeate more fully into the lives of all the members of the church. As part of our own "giving" that the Eucharist sends us out to do as ordained men in the church, we need to "give" our people more opportunity to pray the Liturgy of the Hours with us and more facility in praying it effectively.

"*Giving*" With, Not Merely "*Giving*" To

This admonition for priests and deacons to include more of the people we serve in our praying the Divine Office reminds us that any liturgy is never something that exclusively claims the ordained so that the ordained can do sacred things *for* God's people and give sacred things *to* God's people. Instead, the inclusion of others in the Liturgy of the Hours reminds us that all liturgy, most especially the Eucharist and every form of prayer that enhances the Eucharist, claims us *with* God's people so that *in the midst of* God's people we can give energy and sustenance to everyone in the church being claimed by the eucharistic narrative of Jesus Christ.

Think about the parallels to this: A priest is not ordained to offer the sacrifice of Christ at the altar so that no one else has to offer any sacrifice in their lives to God or for the sake of God's people; nor is a priest ordained to preach the Word of God so that the other members of the church never have to spread the gospel in their lives. Keep in mind that by virtue of baptism all the members of the church share in the priestly and prophetic offices of Christ. This means that they are called to join their lives to the self-offering of Christ in praise and thanksgiving to God, to give witness to the Word of God by letting the power of the gospel shine through their lives, and to evangelize the world.[16] This is referred to variously as "the priesthood of all the baptized," "the priesthood of the faithful" or "the priestly community."[17]

Similarly, a deacon is not ordained to serve the needs of the poor or visit the sick or imprisoned so that the rest of the members of the church do not have to do these most sacred things. All the baptized and confirmed members of the church are called and commissioned into what might be called "the diaconate of all the baptized" or "the common diaconate." This means that all the members of the church are meant to serve the needs of others, especially those on the margins of life. To deny this would be to reject Christ's teaching in his final parable of the sheep and the goats in which those who care for the hungry, thirsty, naked, ill, stranger, and imprisoned are in actuality caring for Christ's presence and, therefore, will be accepted into the kingdom of heaven.[18]

---

16. See especially Vatican II's *Lumen Gentium,* 34 and 35.

17. *Lumen Gentium*, 11.

18. See Matt 25:31-46.

This brings us back to a theological concept mentioned earlier: Deacons and priests are ordained to live with *magnetic density* what *all* the baptized and confirmed members of the church are called to live. Hence, what we "give" in our ministry as deacons and priests is never a paternalistic "giving to" the people something we have exclusive access to; that is, it never arises out of having something of God they do not have and so we will graciously offer it to them. Instead, our ministry is more of an evocative "giving with" our people; that is, we are to draw out from our people what we are all to offer together as a eucharistic people striving to live the eucharistic way of life. As we deacons and priests are claimed more and more by the eucharistic narrative we celebrate so often, we are to draw all of our people into that same process of being claimed by the Holy Spirit to: (1) "take/receive" the lives, the church, the world we have been given and be attentive to how God is with us in all the particularities we experience; (2) "bless" God with thankful hearts for all that God is for us in what we experience; (3) enter into the communion of the "broken" Christ with our own brokenness and the brokenness of the church and the world; (4) in order to receive Christ's broken body and poured out blood in Holy Communion so that we can "give" ourselves to the church and to the world as the tangible presence of Christ for all.

With all the baptized and confirmed, the ordained give themselves eucharistically to the church and to the world. This means that we will need to "give" our people example, instructions, encouragement, challenge, and consolation in their efforts to live the eucharistic way of life and their capacity to "give" themselves as the presence of Christ to the people and circumstances of their particular lives. This is so much more than merely coming to Mass and "getting the goods" (i.e., enjoying the music, hearing a good homily, or receiving Communion) so that everyone can get back to their lives and nothing changes in the parish; nothing is made better in the larger world; no lives are touched or transformed; no works of mercy are performed; no spiritual lives are made deeper; no Christian witness is offered; and no love of God is given to broken lives in a broken world. As deacons and priests, we need energetically to give ourselves over to the Eucharist so that our eucharistic people will powerfully and effectively give themselves to the mission of the church in the world. Borrowing from the Gospel of John quoted at the beginning of this chapter, for God so loved the world that he gave us his only Son; God continues lovingly to give the world his Son in and through all of us as eucharistic people.

Prayer and Reflection (Option A)

Take a few moments of silent reflection.
Prayerfully ponder the following:

1. Ask the Holy Spirit to unite you to the self-emptying heart and will of Christ.

2. What are some ways that you have given yourself to the people of God that has made you feel most connected to Christ the deacon or Christ the priest?

3. Give to God your thankful heart for those moments

4. What are some ways that you are asked to give of yourself in ministry that you struggle with the most? How does this connect with your own brokenness?

5. Ask Christ, who is intimately united to your brokenness, to unite you to his capacity to give to God and to God's people.

6. Pray the Canticle of Ephesians 2:5-11 from Sunday Evening Prayer I.

Prayer and Reflection (Option B)

Take a few moments of silent reflection.
Prayerfully ponder the following:

1. Ask the Holy Spirit for wisdom, knowledge and understanding.

2. What are some ways that you have ministered with your people in giving of yourselves to the mission of the church?

3. Give to God your thankful heart for those moments.

4. What are some ways that you ought to evoke from your people in relation to their giving to some aspect of the church's mission that needs to improve in your parish or place of ministry?

5. Sit in silence with Christ and ask him to share how he evoked a sense of mission from his disciples.

6. Pray Christ's prayer for his disciples in John 17.

Epilogue

What if a Story Became Your Life?

As the plotline of the film *Stranger Than Fiction* progresses, the lead character, Harold Cricks, eventually finds the author, Karen Eiffel, whose voice he has been hearing in his head narrating what is about to happen in his life, including his imminent tragic death. Harold asks Karen to spare his life. Struggling to find her composure upon discovering that the main character in her supposedly fictional novel is a real-life person, Karen looks at him intently and stammers to offer a response. She knows that the tragic ending she has already planned for her novel about Harold is the only fitting ending to the story; it is the best ending. As Harold continues to plead with Karen, he is given a preliminary copy that details the sad conclusion for the story—his story. After Harold reads it, he too realizes it is the best possible ending and he tells Karen to finish writing it as she planned. Yet now, Harold's assent to knowingly meet his terrible fate alters the true character evidenced so far in the novel's protagonist. In the estimation of the future readers of the story (cleverly captured by the reactions of the current viewers of the film) Harold is revealed as so much more than they ever realized. He becomes a much more noble and compelling figure at the end of the novel because he allowed himself to be claimed so fully by the entire plot of the novel. When the story truly became his life, Harold truly became the man he was always meant to be.

Our true story makes us who we are meant to be. Despite all the unexpected joys and surprises, the unforeseen tragedies and sorrows, the unanticipated events and circumstances of a person's life, the personal story of any Christian man or woman can never be described as simply as a plot "stranger than fiction." More accurately, the life of any disciple is "better than fiction" when it is claimed by the story of Jesus Christ. To that end, the narrative voice of the Holy Spirit constantly beckons us to let the story of Jesus become our lives because it is the true and authentic story of who we are meant to be. It is the best story. This is true for all disciples of Christ; that the story of Jesus is the only story that can write our personal narratives. Unlike the movie in which Harold Crick seemed to be completely at the mercy of some outside "author" of his life, the Spirit always writes the narrative of our lives in conjunction with our faith and free will. As deacons and priests, when our free will surrenders into the story of Jesus we have come to believe in deeply, we become the ordained men we are meant to be. As Jesus' story is inherently eucharistic, so too our story must be. As the narrative of Jesus culminates in a climactic self-emptying and a complete self-giving, so must we allow the Holy Spirit to write those narrative elements in our own lives and in the ministries we exercise on behalf of God's people. Borrowing the tagline from the advertising for *Stranger Than Fiction* cited at the beginning of this text, the eucharistic story is to become our life.

Letting a story become our life involves so much more than being able to read and recognize the sequential progression of the narrative from one plot point to the next until it reaches its ultimate conclusion. To be claimed by a story involves giving ourselves into the story. What all of this makes clear is that if the eucharistic narrative of Jesus is to become our life, then it is never enough to make the Eucharist only something we *celebrate* in our communities of ministry, even if celebrated with fervor and devotion; it is never enough for the Eucharist to be something we *bring* to the sick, the homebound, or the imprisoned, even if we bring it with compassion and kindness; it is never enough for the Eucharist to be a subject we *teach and preach* about, even when done so with zeal and conviction. The narrative that is to claim us is not complete until we *live* the Eucharist vividly and authentically in every aspect of who we are as followers of Christ and in everything we offer God's people as deacons and priests. Living the Eucharist happens only by giving ourselves into a compelling relationship with a person, Jesus Christ. It is Jesus who, in knowing us so intimately, beckons us to know him personally and deeply. It is Jesus who, in giving us his very self, draws us into his own narrative of self-giving. It is Jesus who, in wanting us to become the persons he knows us to be, calls all the baptized to a vocation of authentic discipleship which, for deacons and priests, includes the vocation to ordained ministry within the church.

A true vocation is never a self-generated reality. Precisely because it is a "calling" (the Latin *vocare* means "to call"), it comes from a source other than just the one being called. For us as Christians, we believe that the One who calls is never an anonymous voice that has no identity; it is always the Holy Spirit speaking the Word, that is, the sacred narrative of the person of Jesus Christ who lives the story he is trying to write with our lives. What this means is that a Christian vocation, *any truly Christian vocation*, is a calling to live something *with* Jesus. Since the narrative of Jesus involves both a priestly dimension and a diaconal dimension, then those in holy orders are together to live with *magnetic density* the two interwoven plotlines within Jesus' narrative in order to help animate all the members of the church to live the priestly and diaconal story of Christ. The vocation of a priest is a calling to live the priestly narrative of Jesus—a narrative of surrendering one's life into Christ's self-offering in praise and thanksgiving to the Father that happens in and through Christ's sacred communion with all that is broken in human lives and in the world. The vocation of a deacon is a calling to live the diaconal narrative of Jesus—a narrative of surrendering one's life into Christ's humble service to the people of God as the self-emptying of God's love into the world.

When a man feels called to the diaconate or priesthood, it can never be approached merely as a vocation of self-discovery in which one comes to know what he is to do to achieve a life of self-fulfillment. Where's the *breaking* and *giving* in that? Instead, a vocation is always a Spirit-guided journey *with* Christ and *in* Christ in which one discerns how best to live the eucharistic narrative of Christ, which always allows one's *breaking* to become a generative *giving*. For that discernment to happen authentically and effectively, one needs to come to know deeply and personally Jesus the servant (the deacon) and Jesus the priest so as to be claimed by his story. Admittedly, one also needs to know oneself well and one needs to be intimately familiar with how the voice of the Spirit has sounded in one's own depths. Both of these dimensions of discernment are revealed through learning to read one's life correctly, or perhaps better, though learning to listen well to one's own personal narrative that has transpired thus far.

Many priests and deacons after some time in ordained ministry become quite disillusioned with their vocational choice. Unfortunately, too many of them then walk away from the priesthood or diaconate. It is my contention that more often than not (but not always) this decision is premature and not well-discerned. First of all, the disillusionment about being ordained comes from wanting the *giving* of one's life to eliminate any sense of brokenness within a person's life; that somehow getting ordained was to eliminate all the forms of disappointment or deficiencies in one's life. Secondly, the disillusionment about one's chosen vocation also arises from not really knowing the true narrative of Christ the priest or Christ the deacon. Besides the joy and fulfillment that Christ must have found in his public ministry, he also experienced failure, frustration, loneliness, limited results, hostile reactions, and indifference. Thus, we need to be careful that we define experientially and not just ideally the priesthood and diaconate of Christ. Idealized theological notions of what it means to be a deacon or priest might certainly inspire a man in his discovery of a vocation to ordained ministry and spur him on to live out that vocation. But eventually, even that idealized narrative of priesthood or diaconate has to be claimed by the very realities within the gospel narratives of Jesus' public life and ministry, including that it all led to his suffering and death.

Both of these erroneous ways of processing disillusionment stem from the same wrongful expectation: that there can be *giving* without *breaking,* thus not really allowing oneself to be claimed by the eucharistic narrative of Jesus. But there is also a third error in dealing with disillusionment and disappointment in ministry that runs deeper than the failure to live *breaking* authentically and offer vocational *giving* rightly. It comes from never having learned how to do the *taking* and *blessing* of our lives in the first place. Often this deficiency manifests itself long after we have been trying to live the lives we have felt called to live, when we begin to feel that the life we have chosen does not "fit" us well. Admittedly, there can be instances when there actually was a wrong choice in vocation, but I contend that in many cases it is a matter of not having yet learned what one's life story has been revealing all along. It is a failure to read well the narrative of one's life or to listen attentively to what the story of one's life has been speaking long before the present disillusionment or disappointment surfaced. We read rightly or listen well to our own lives when we *take* them rightly with careful attentiveness to how they have been manifestations of God-with-us in all the particular events, experiences, and persons that have shaped the narrative thus far, the good as well as the bad. Then we *bless* God with deep gratitude for all that God has been for us in the entire story that has brought us to the present moment in our lives; again, in the good as well as the bad. These aspects of *taking* and *blessing* are necessary preconditions for a vocational discernment that leads to *breaking* and *giving*. If they were not done well before a vocational discernment was made, this does not necessarily mean that a wrong vocation was chosen. Frequently it indicates that one has not yet learned how to live one's life authentically. Therefore, it is not the vocation that does not fit; it is the false narrative of one's self that is off kilter. In order to *take* and *bless* our true lives, we have to let our lives speak to us.

The spiritual author Parker Palmer writes well about the old Quaker adage "Let your life speak." He counsels that we often have to adjust our way of thinking about what it means to come to a sense of vocation by not listening only to the highest ideals that keep surfacing inside of us nor to the stories of the most noble heroes we keep wanting to emulate. This often reduces our sense of vocation to something our ego wills to achieve for ourselves.[19] Palmer warns:

> Vocation does not come from willfulness. It comes from listening. I must listen to my life and try to understand what it is truly about—quite apart from what I would like it to be about—or my life will never represent anything real in the world, no matter how earnest my intentions. . . . Vocation does not mean a goal that I pursue. It means a calling that I hear. Before I can tell my life what I want to do with it, I must listen to my life telling me who I am. I must listen to the truths and values at the heart of my own identity, not the standards by which I *must* live—but the standards by which I cannot help but live if I am living my own life.[20]

In terms of discerning vocation, or more properly in discerning how to live authentically the vocation one has already been living, Parker speaks a truth we all need to hear but often fail to listen to in the enthusiasm of our idealized sense of ourselves and our goal. He states:

> Everyone has a life that is different from the "I" of daily consciousness, a life that is trying to live through the "I" who is its vessel. This is what the poet knows and what every wisdom tradition teaches: there is a great gulf between the way my ego wants to identify me, with its protective masks and self-serving

---

19. Parker Palmer, *Let Your Life Speak: Listening for the Voice of Vocation* (San Francisco: Jossey-Bass, 2000), 3–4.
20. Palmer, 4–5.

fictions, and my true self. It takes time and hard experience to sense the difference between the two—to sense that running beneath the surface of the experience I call my life, there is a deeper and truer life waiting to be acknowledged.[21]

That deeper and truer life that beckons deep inside of us is the narrative of Jesus who knows us better than we know ourselves. It is a life that can never be lived apart from the intimacy with Christ that leads us through each successive chapter in our lives. It is the life of Christ that is always seeking to live in us in such a way that it brings tremendous grace to our lives: comfort and hope in difficult times; thanksgiving and joy in moments of happiness; wisdom and companionship when we are not sure where the story is leading or what the story means; challenge and reassurance when we have lost track of the true narrative that ought to define us; and, finally, courage and strength when the story becomes painful, even tragic. When vocational disillusionment and disappointment set in for deacons and priests, before we want to change the story of our lives, we need to first ask if we have been letting the true story of our lives live in us.

This true story speaking to our lives and trying to speak through our lives, as we have explored throughout this book, is necessarily a eucharistic narrative precisely because it is the narrative of Jesus. Thus, it is always a story in which unfolds a graced manner of *taking, blessing, breaking,* and *giving.* Like any good story, it needs to be heard and then entered into by the hearer. It is a story inscribed in all Christian persons at baptism. It is a sacred saga that disciples of Jesus are empowered to live at confirmation. It is a narrative that speaks an additional vocation and challenge to deacons and priests, calling them to live the story in such a vivid way that it draws all the baptized and confirmed into the awareness that the same story of Jesus seeks to live in them and in the world around them.

---

21. Palmer, 5.

As deacons and priests, are you and I living the story of Jesus with the vividness and authenticity to which we have been called? Perhaps not yet; there might still need to be a lot more sublating of our hearts, minds, and wills to the eucharistic heart, mind, and will of Christ. However, let us never forget that our ordination was not the end of the Holy Spirit claiming us for the diaconal story and priestly story of Jesus. Remember that at our ordination, after we made all of our pledges and promises to the bishop, the bishop then said to us, "May God who has begun the good work in you bring it to fulfillment." What a wonderful invocation from the bishop that permeates all the years we live as an ordained deacon or priest. It is a clear statement that no matter how long we have been ordained, no matter how often we have celebrated the Eucharist, no matter how much we have struggled or succeeded in ministry, God is not yet done with us. The Holy Spirit continues to write the eucharistic narrative of Jesus inside of us so that it claims, sometimes with gusto but often with subtlety, more and more of what we are to live. Imagine, just imagine, if we truly allowed that story to become our life!

Closing Prayer and Reflection (Option A)

Take a few moments of silent reflection.
Prayerfully ponder the following:

1. Read one of the following institution narratives:
   - 1 Corinthians 11:23-26
   - Mark 14:22-26
   - Matthew 26:26-30
   - Luke 22:14-20

2. What words or actions of Jesus within the eucharistic narrative claim you the most? Why?

3. What words or actions of Jesus within the eucharistic narrative challenge you the most? Why?

4. As you consider the above questions, what might Christ be revealing to you about yourself?

5. What might Christ be summoning from you as a deacon or priest?

6. End your prayer and reflection by praying Psalm 116.

Closing Prayer and Reflection (Option B)

Take a few moments of silent reflection.
Prayerfully ponder the following:

1. Choose your favorite eucharistic prayer.

2. Pray with it in the manner of *lectio divina.*
   - What words, phrases or images speak to you the most?
   - Sit with one or two of them for a while.

3. What does the prayer say to you about the eucharistic nature of your vocation?

4. What part of the prayer speaks a word of challenge to you?

5. What part of the prayer offers you a sense of being energized for ministry?

6. End by praying the eucharistic prayer out loud.